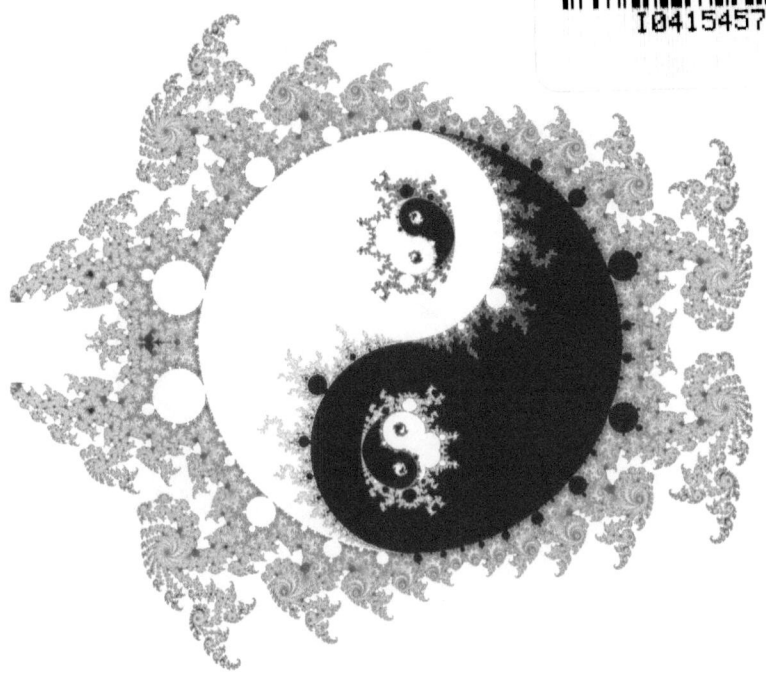

Trans Experiences

A Research Report For Trans Communities And Their Allies

Second Edition

Eva C. Moser

The content of this book is available for download at www.evamoser.ca/research.
This book is also available in e-pub format as ISBN 978-1-304-16089-8.

Trans Experiences

Dedicated to all those who have suffered

because imposing compliance to structures, beliefs,

rules and orders was deemed more important

than acknowledging their humanity and their lives

Published by Lulu Press

860 Aviation Parkway, Suite 300

Morrisville, NC 27560

www.lulu.com - lulu-id 13269293

V2-2.4[11]E@19071

1. Transsexuality, 2. Transgender, 3. Human Rights

ISBN-13: 978-1-300-27860-3

Yin/Yang Fractal cover-design copyright © 2013 Eva C. Moser

Acknowledgments

I would like to thank my partner for accepting me as I am; I would like to thank her for her compassion, her love, her support and her sharing her life with me. I would like to thank our children, they have been and are my inspiration for life! I would like to thank all of them for giving me the many hours to conduct this study and write this book, I know they missed me just as I missed them. I love you all so very much!

I would like to thank York University for giving me the opportunity to participate in their Masters of Social Work program. The survey and research this report is based on was carried out as a part of this program in the form of a Practice Research Paper. I would like to thank the faculty, staff and students of the School of Social Work for their support and for an outstanding learning experience over the past 2 years. My thanks also go out to Prof. Dr. Andrea Daley who represented York University in the position of graduate supervisor for the PRP this report is based on.

My gratitude goes out to the staff and volunteers of The 519 Church Street Community Centre, and The Centre For Women And Trans People at York University, for their support in promoting the original research, for their encouragement and kindness.

For editing and critical feedback my thanks go out to Chris Veldhoven. His review of my language, grammar and the structure of the document will benefit every reader. The many hours of discussion we had on topics covered by my research were a great pleasure. They helped me to locate myself and to push forward with questioning the status quo, present new ideas more clearly, and put challenging discourses into a larger context.

A very special thank you goes out to all the members of our trans communities, the people who have shared some of their lives with me in this research, the people I personally know, and all the wonderful people I have yet to meet. Thank you. You are amazing!

Foreword

This report is based on the survey and research I carried out as a Practice Research Paper[59] from January to April 2013 for my M.S.W. at York University in Toronto, Canada.

It is a small first step, investigating something - trans self-experience and self-identification - that warrants a much larger investment. However, I hope to come back to the topic in the future, expand and build on this research, and provide trans communities with a more detailed and in-depth analysis of who we really are. Trans people and communities deserve nothing less!

As a practice research paper, the original paper and survey this report is based on had to follow academic formatting. As often required in academic writing, there was a restriction on the total length of the paper. The original paper also had to include theoretical sections such as an extensive discussion of the existing literature, the theoretical interpretation used, the design of the survey, and the methodology. Brief summaries of these parts are provided in this report to give background information. Expansions on these parts can be found in the original paper[59].

Writing this community report allows me to examine the complexities of some of the findings in more depth in a more open format, and to report findings that could not be included in the research paper due the aforementioned limitations on time and length. Many issues faced by trans and genderqueer people are complex in the face of living in restrictive and fearful gendered beliefs and cultures. Often, addressing this complexity requires new perspectives. Trans community perspectives force everyone to step back and question themselves, just as trans/genderqueer people have questioned themselves and their own lives for eons. Such perspectives can't be definitely addressed in a single paper, or even in a report that is not limited in length. But this study can be a start. It can be a step towards a better understanding of our lives, our communities and, ultimately, of ourselves.

A Personal Retrospective

As I write this, it has been 3 months since the survey this research is based upon has closed, yet I continue to receive requests to participate by e-mail. Some people ask if they really are too late, others provide me with responses to the main research question, *how they themselves describe being trans,* in their e-mails.

Unfortunately, I can't accept this data for research purposes as receiving it through e-mail instead of through the online survey would circumvent obtaining consent from participants in the form that had been designated in the process of ethics approval by York University for the original research. Having said this, I do of course read e-mails that are sent to me, and I will include what I learn in the design of subsequent research and writings.

The fact that I still receive submissions, months after the survey has closed and without asking for any, shows me - more than anything else ever could - that members of trans communities are not only eager to participate, but that there is a real need to express themselves within the context of community based scientific research. Community responses have been absolutely amazing.

Contents

1

PROLOGUE

1.1 A Question Yet To Be Answered

Being trans is a form of self-interpretation, self-experience and self-expression. Therefore, to understand trans people's lives, their experiences of being trans must be studied. Some authors of professional literature (e.g. clinicians, counsellors, psychologists,...) include passages on how transsexuals describe their own experience of being transsexual, but this is usually limited to incidental side-notes and, in older publications, to speculations and assumptions based on very limited data[1,4,28,53]. The deficit oriented interpretation of transsexuality as a pathology, established by the medical system, prevails in the more contemporary professional literature[2,6,54,55,77,79,80,82,83]. But the medical interpretation, embodied by the DSM's "Gender Identity Disorder" [GID, see A.3, *The DSM's Gender Identity Disorder*], allows for only one 'pathology' with a very limited range of self-interpretations[1,2,79,80]. This leads to a treatment model which implies a combination of sexual motivations (which are often assumed to be of an auto-erotic nature) and social (e.g. 'lifestyle') motivations and expressions.

Through this view of 'disorder', self-interpretation, self-experience and self-expression become prescriptive assumptions of the theoretical model (psychiatric or psychological), employed to explain the behaviours seen in patients. Or, in other words: if an individual fails to show the expected 'symptoms' of transsexuality, then that person is not a transsexual, and thus does not 'require' (or deserve) any related treatment(s).

While the above is written by people who have been influenced by an education to interpret the world in a pathological way, people who write their own stories free from pathologizing influences paint a completely different picture of how they experience themselves. These descriptions are typically sophisticated, often extensive in length, detailed and multi-faceted[15,56,61,71,73,74]. Some of these authors address professionally inferred self-experiences and usually reject them.

The discrepancy between professional literature and public, non-scientific sources suggests that there is a major disconnect between historical and contemporary professional writing and the range of self-expressions from trans people themselves[57,58]. To date, there has been no systematic research on the experiences of transsexuality by actual members of trans communities. This report will address this gap by asking *how do transsexuals describe their own experiences of transsex-*

17

uality in the form of a question to a friend, and then reporting on the diversity and complexity expressed by respondents.

1.1.1   The Survey

For many individuals in trans communities, *privacy* is of utmost concern. While some live publicly as trans, others may not be fully 'out' and share their identity only with a small group of friends. Some have fully transitioned and live publicly without disclosing their previous lives (this is also known as 'living stealth'). In both cases fear of disclosure, even to a researcher who promises anonymity, may prevent individuals from participating. The possibility of accidental disclosure, for example by being seen with the researcher, could be detrimental.

These concerns were addressed by using an anonymous internet based survey to collect data, thus eliminating any contact between the researcher and the participant, and any knowledge by the researcher of who participated. This method is widely accepted in the research of gender communities [examples include: NTCE & NGLTF (2009, 2010)[63,64]; TransPluse (2009)[76]; Greatheart (2010)[30]; Singh et al. (2011)[72]; Kerrigan (2011)[41]; Dispenza et al. (2012)[17]]. In the interest of participant anonymity, no personal data such as name, place of residence or date of birth was collected.

The survey contained a consent section, a demographics section and a quantitative section on medical treatment and transition. The questions in these sections were consistent with the much larger TransPulse[76] (2009) and the NTDS[63,64] surveys, to allow for a comparison of the participating populations. The main question of the research consisted of a qualitative question that asked participants to provide a short description of their experiences of transsexuality in 150 words or less. This was followed by questions, on the participation in clinical surveys. The survey concluded with a referral page asking participants to invite other members of trans communities to participate (to initiate 'chain-referral' sampling[A]).

The aim was to collect at least 40 completed responses. Ultimately, 48 participants completed the survey in the 2 weeks of data collection.

[A] *'Chain-referral sampling', also known as 'snowball sampling' is a technique where participants of a study invite other participants among their acquaintances. The advantage of this form of participant invitation is that the researcher does not need to directly invite (or know) all participants and that there is a certain control to keep participation within the study group. The major disadvantage is that it does not provide a statistically neutral sample. For example, people with many friends are more likely to be invited than people with few or no friends.*

1.1.2 Participants

One of the goals of the original project was to compare self-identified descriptions of being trans with assumptions presented in the clinical literature. However, clinicians to date have not arrived at a consensus about who to include in the definition of trans (or transsexual) and who to exclude. Consequently various clinical publications will base their research on vastly different populations under this umbrella. Even the medical *Standards Of Care* [SOC] acknowledge that within various studies the interpretation of the term transsexual differs so widely "in their criteria for documenting a person as transsexual" that "direct comparisons across studies are impossible"[80].

Given this discrepancy in the clinical literature, it was important for my research to invite only individuals who would be included as 'being trans' even under the most stringent of criteria. If I then find anything statistically significant that is not represented in the clinical literature, I can reasonably argue that clinicians should have also at least noticed what I find, as the people, self-identifications and self-expressions found in my survey must, statistically, also be represented in their research populations. Consequently, only individuals who had obtained, were in the process of obtaining, or consider medical interventions such as trans related hormonal treatment or surgeries (most notably SRS), were invited.

I personally strongly disagree with a definition of people as transsexual as a result of a clinical pathology and believe that any form of being trans must remain self-identified and cannot be assigned by a third party, just as sexual orientation is self-identified and not assigned by a medical practitioner. However, if I would invite individuals to participate according to their self-identification, then clinicians would simply make the argument that my research is based on a different population (e.g. people they never see), and thus is not comparable. This would also mean that any criticism would not be applicable.

As mentioned, convenience sampling (direct invitation of eligible participants known by the researcher) and chain-referral sampling were used to invite participants. Invitations were sent through e-mail, posted in social media and given in trans groups and programs. Invitations remained within trans communities and did not involve clinical professionals.

1.2 *Where Is The Author*

While I am often called *trans* or *transsexual* by people who believe to know me, and I sometimes use these terms to describe my journey, I neither identify with the term nor believe that it actually is a meaningful description of who I am. Nevertheless, 'transsexual' is the best commonly recognized term to acknowledge that society believes, expertly declares and legally insists, 'I have experienced some form of gender transition'. Instead, I prefer the term *human* as a self-identification, or, if pressured for a gendered designation for some reason, I will settle for *woman* or *female*.

I may have accepted *transsexual* as a reasonably accurate description of myself before SRS, when an inconsistency between my self-experience and my sexual function actually existed, as the term implies, but I do not consider the term relevant to who I am today.

1.2.1 *Being Different*

My journey began early in life with a clear *feeling of female preference.* However I never experienced significant social or emotional problems with my gender role prior to coming out. While I clearly preferred to self-express in an androgynous way and have always refused 'male dress-up' or 'power-dressing', I now do the same in my current female role. However, even early in life I did feel a profound inability to experience, express and share emotions, compared to what I would have deemed meaningful. For example, I was crying inside, but my body refused to project this to the outside with tears. During puberty, this experience increased to a brutal limitation. Meanwhile, except for myself, nobody ever seemed to notice that I identified differently, with the occasional social interpretation that I might be an 'effeminate' gay male. During all this time any experience of my own sexuality was nonexistent.

I clearly felt that I needed treatment; in particular HRT for a fulfilling emotional self-experience and fulfilling self-expression, and SRS to potentially gain the experience of physical sexuality. Yet none of what I experienced can be found in the diagnostic standards of the SOC nor anywhere in the DSM[2]. I would have *preferred* to socially grow-up, live and be acknowledged as being female, but I never experienced "gender dysphoria" as described in the DSM[2]. Instead, I accepted my previous social role. I certainly did not live a typically male life as a full-time caregiver to our children, yet I never actually felt a need to socially transition. Of course not qualifying for anything according to these existing 'professional standards' meant that I was not eligible for any form of treatment whatsoever.

Ultimately, my frustration at my inability to express emotions became so severe that I no longer minded to lie my way through the system to feel whole. I accepted a social gender transition that I would not have chosen myself, at least not in that way and at that time. In order to become eligible for the interventions I needed, I submitted to abusive examinations, absurd expectations and emotionally and physically destructive treatments. To put this differently, I was forced to screw-up my life in every respect possible, legally, socially, interpersonally, physically, and yes, emotionally, in order to obtain a permit for continued existence.

Today - in an ingenious reverse conclusion that only mad people can ever get SRS, therefore all people who have obtained SRS must be mad - I now find myself instantly diagnosed mentally ill by every medical practitioner I have seen since, including practitioners who did not even treat me, such as a paediatrician of my children. After all, if only people who are so severely mentally ill that they need to be deprived of the right to make decisions about their own bodies can ever obtain SRS, then I must be utterly mad for virtue of having been given this treatment.

I understand that my personal need for HRT and SRS are not typical for what many individuals in trans communities experience. It is a minority experience within an already small minority. Nevertheless, my experience of the process and of treatment itself is in many ways similar to what everybody else gets subjected.

1.2.2 Researching My Own Communities

Researching one's own communities can be challenging and rewarding. It is always self-reflective in a very specific way. What I research and describe are experiences that have been part of, or are very closely related to, my own life. My experiences have made me who I am; they have given me a place in our communities. But they have also made me experience some things in specific ways, ways others can or can't relate to, ways that may be similar or very dissimilar to other people's experiences.

Taylor reflects on the importance of the in-community researcher relationship with her own work in the "queer community". She notes that this "reshapes the researcher's role in and [her] experiences of her own culture and those within it"[75]. According to Taylor, insider research may have advantages. She notes a "deeper levels of understanding", "being 'empirically literate'" and easier access to better informed research participants[75]. She also lists disadvantages such as "accounts concerning the effectiveness of such 'insider knowledge' remain largely circumspect and anecdotal" and "as an insider, one [does not] necessarily offer an absolute or correct way of seeing and/or reading the culture"[75]. Taylor particularly notes that the "privileging [of] knowledge that is constructed within dichotomous rubrics such as insider/outsider"[75] is problematic.

However, within trans communities terms such as 'insider' and 'outsider' are to some degree meaningless. While one can certainly be an 'outsider' and neither have any idea what being trans is about, nor ever have been affected by any facet of being trans oneself, it is by definition not possible to be 'a true insider' as there are many, highly diverse trans communities. While I am surely an 'insider' of my own community, because of this exceptional diversity, this community of mine becomes very much a small subgroup within a much larger context. In every other community I remain, by definition, at least to some degree an 'outsider'. Or, to put this differently: how we, in trans communities, *get treated* 'by the outside' has always, in my experience, been more of a common experience than *how we experience and define ourselves.* Hence, I am 'an outsider with some shared experiences' to every single one of our communities. Meanwhile, the various, but very significant dissimilarities keep me acutely aware of both the advantages and the disadvantages of my position.

Surely, I will interpret what I find differently than a researcher would who has not lived some form of 'trans experience'. I will give it a distinct 'trans perspective' - my own - which will be different from many others in our communities. I will not be 'more objective' than others who research our communities, I don't even try to be. But I do try to be inclusive of the diversity of trans communities of which I know, a diversity that may just be easier for me to access (but not necessarily to understand or describe) than it is for people who are not subject to being called 'trans'.

For me, there is great value in adding such a perspective, if only for virtue of adding a different interpretation, in particular when seen in combination with perspectives other researchers offer.

Chapter 1: Prologue

Contents

▶ An introduction to the survey this report is based on (1.1).

▶ The position and perspective of the author (1.2).

Conclusions

▶ There is a lack of research on trans people and their communities.

▶ Much of what can be found in the literature is based on assumptions and very little data; findings are often distorted by the interpretation through a clinical and pathologizing lens.

2

HOW WE GOT TO

WHERE WE ARE

2.1 *Positions*

2.1.1 *In- And Exclusion, Terms And Definitions*

Even though the psychiatric community without discrimination pathologizes pretty much the entire 'gender community' through the definition of *gender identity disorder*[2] [GID] and *transvestic fetishism*[2], few people appear on their doorstep to have their 'disorderly conduct' certified as madness. As a result, much of the professional literature is based on relatively few individuals who *do* seek treatment for gender transition. Examples include: Benjamin[1], APA[2,28], WPATH[79,80], Urban[77], Zucker[83,84]. As the psychiatric community declares that such treatment is theirs to grant or deny, individuals who seek it become a convenient 'captive audience'.

Definitions of the terms 'transsexuality' and 'transsexual' seem equally arbitrary. No consensus exists. Hirschfeld was one of the first to define distinct categories that today might be interpreted as describing *some form of transsexuality*[35,37] just after the turn of the century. In 1966 Benjamin defined the still widely referred to *Benjamin Scale*[4], which differentiates between 'transvestitism', 'non-surgical' transsexuality, and two 'intensities' of 'surgical' transsexuality. His interpretation of transsexuality was that of 'a more severe form of transvestic fetishism' or a 'sexual perversion'.

Later definitions included the non-fetishistic adaptation that transsexuality is a subcategory of the newly coined term 'transgender', whereas 'transgender' refers to any form of (visual) transgression of 'gender norms'. Today various authors interchangeably use the term transsexual as a synonym for: 'transgender', people who seek some form of medical treatment, individuals who are 'diagnosed with GID' and so forth. As mentioned before, the medical Standards Of Care [SOC] admits that interpretations of the term transsexual within studies differ so widely that direct comparisons across studies are impossible[80].

For the purpose of this study I will use the terms *trans* to describe members of the larger communities, and *transsexual* for: anybody *who is subject to the SOC's restrictions to access medical care*[79,80]: individuals who consider, seek or use hormonal treatment [HRT]; or individuals who consider, seek or have had any of the surgeries the SOC regulates.

I will furthermore use the terms *'sex'* to describe the first designation of male or female assigned to an individual by an authorized 'expert', usually at or just after birth, and *'gender'* to refer to an individual's respective self-interpretation without limitation. This is in line with many community authors, but differs significantly from the clinical use where it is sometimes claimed that *'gender'* is a part of self-identification, but it remains implied that any clinically recognized self-identification is assessed and assigned by a professional or according to a belief-system, which of course makes it *an externally assigned parameter rather than a true and free self-identification*[56]. Consequently, depending upon the assessor's beliefs, the truthfulness of any self-identification that deviates from the individual's previously assessed sex may be accepted on a case by case basis in the form of a clinical diagnosis[4,6,28,43,49,54,82,83], or it may be rejected under any and all circumstances based on a non-accepting belief-system[66,67].

2.1.2 A Fundamental Problem

At this time, professional explanations of transsexuality, and with it any inferred self-experience(s) and motivation(s), are derived from observations collected by medical and psychotherapeutic practitioners when treating patients, rather than from actual research in trans communities. Predictably, Lurkhur finds: "whereas medicine responds to transsexual's claims of being wrongly embodied by attempting to recreate their bodies, psychoanalysts attempt to reconcile transsexuals to the reality of their flesh[sic]"[47].

That surgeons on one side, and psychologists and psychiatrists on the other locate 'the right intervention' in their respective theoretical frameworks appears opportunistic and shows a significant lack of criticism towards their own, very one-sided frames of reference. It is a paternalistic and entirely subjective interpretation formed by professional theory, not facts. Most significantly, it is derived without any regard to the self-identifications or actual expressed needs of the people these professionals in fact 'treat'.

Of course if the question were if transsexuality should be interpreted as a mental illness with need for psychological/psychiatric intervention, or as a physical condition with need for medical/surgical intervention, then science, which is claimed to be the basis for the medical system and model, would offer the perfect way out: a controlled study in the form of a clinical trial. Let a few individuals go on HRT *at their sole discretion* with professionals providing only *educating and monitoring,* but not deciding on timing and interventions (e.g. hormones and suppressants used, and their dosage). Then compare the levels of satisfaction with: (a) a group that is on HRT, but not allowed self-determination in regard to substances and dosages (which, at this time, is everybody who gets treatment by a licensed medical professional), and (b) a group whose members don't get any HRT and are 'told to wait' until they can be granted access to HRT (which, at this time, is everybody subject to the SOC's or to additional institutional 'waiting times'). This should quickly create clarity as to which model is better, or potentially *which model is better for which group of patients.* The fact that (a) even such a simple trial has never taken place and (b) rumours that potentially hundreds of thousands of individuals self-medicate HRT from the black market without creating any negative headlines (e.g. emergency room visits or cause of death) speaks volumes[58].

Sadly, since the inception of medical control of transsexual lives, the goal does not appear to be the provision of the best possible care to trans people (the glaring absence of scientific research and clinical trials clearly shows this), but rather how to best socially control trans people through medical means. This isn't helped if the medical community itself appears to be engaged in an internal feud as to which branch of medicine is entitled to enforce such control: general practice and surgery, or psychiatry. This provides the perfect guarantee that within the context of this struggle of control, the people who actually ought to have control over their own lives, trans people themselves, would never be given any consideration.

At this time access to medical treatment for trans treatment remains defined in the dichotomy of the aforementioned two professional spheres, the psychological-psychiatric approach versus the surgical approach. Obviously, the ability of trans people who need medical interventions to self-express and self-realize is limited by their ability to obtain such treatment. As such, trans people's self-expression and, at least in part, their self-identifications become intricately linked to theoretical and professional interpretations and power struggles, rather than to the actual experiences and needs of individuals[56,57,58].

2.2 *From History To Status Quo*

2.2.1 *Once Upon A Time*

Throughout history several activities were known that today would require treatment controlled by the SOC. The framework outlined in the SOC[79,80] and the DSM[2] allows only for social cross-gender behaviour (e.g. relating to the social role of an individual) and sexual cross-gender behaviour (e.g. relating to the expression of sexual desires through the bio-mechanical sexual function of an individual), no other motivations such as emotional, physical, spiritual or self-realization are mentioned or accepted. Nevertheless, even this limited interpretation of cross-gender behaviour has been documented widely throughout history. Lurkhur for example examines the 13th century novel *Le Roman de Silence* and finds both forced as well as freely assumed long term cross-gender expressions[47]. Blanton & Cook and Gansler document females who enrolled in the Civil War as males and while many historians argue that individuals crossed gender roles solely for the purpose of participating for their cause (as back then the military only accepted male soldiers), this argument hardly holds true for individuals who maintained their male identities for life[7,29].

A very different type of transition can be found in the tradition of voluntary castration. This is documented throughout history, in spiritual texts in particular. The King James Bible from 1611 for example offers this reference: "For there are some eunuchs which were so borne [...] and there are some eunuchs which were made eunuchs of men; *and there be eunuchs, which have made themselves eunuchs*"[42,emphasis added]. The passage further states that this choice should be honoured and supported (Matthew 19:12[42,A]).

While we do not know why individuals asked to be emasculated, we do know that *as a procedure requested by a patient,* a 'castration' (or orchiectomy) today is restricted to people who qualify under the SOC[79,80] to receive trans related treatment. The procedure is interpreted as *a partial feminization* of the male body. We also know that terms such as *living "on a testosterone horror trip"*[56,emphasis added] are used by some members of trans communities to describe their experience of the emotional impact of the male sex hormone testosterone at 'biologically

---

[A] *Some editions, including the Revised Standard Version[69] used by the Catholic Church, translate this passage very differently.*

normal male levels'. Consequently, practices such as self-orchiectomies (as a self-treatment to reduce the biological levels and effects of testosterone) are well known in some communities.[A]

Meanwhile, it is interesting to note that while some medical professionals stead-fastly deny the possibility of a personality based or neurological preference for male or female sex hormones, other practitioners use similar steroids to change personal-ity-related features in foetuses. Dreger et al. document that treatment with steroids "has been aimed at preventing development of ambiguous genitalia, the urogenital sinus, *tomboyism, and lesbianism*"[18,emphasis added], and of course no approval by the SOC or any other medical or psychiatric standard is necessary to obtain *treatment to prevent lesbianism*. On one hand, professionals argue that a non-consensual application of steroids will change an individual's personality in a very dramatic way. On the other hand, the argument is made that a voluntary need for treatment with very similar substances (e.g. sex hormones) to align one's self-experience with one's personality can never exist. One would think that if the involuntary procedure is known to work, that then the existence of a voluntary equivalent can at least not be denied outright, in particular without the benefit of any research.

After the turn of the century Hirschfeld saw gender as a multidimensional contin-uum. He particularly included biochemical (hormonal) aspects of gender[35,36,37]. Ekins finds that in his early works in the 1950's, Benjamin, one of the first North American medical practitioners to provide services to trans communities, retained a social *as well as* a biological motivation for transsexuality[20]. However, he never describes spiritual motivations. Modern representations of this dualism in the literature include Elliot[21]and Namaste. The latter distinguishes *transgender* individuals (who *socially* cross gender norms) and *transsexuals* (who *biologically* cross gender norms), stating that *transsexuals* are distinct and should not be included in the (larger) *transgender* population[61,62]. Namaste also maintains that *transsexuals* usually have little interest in questioning identity[62].

My own interpretation is more fluid. Social transition *may* include biological changes (not limited to the socially normative), while physical transition *may* include a social expression (not limited to the medically normative)[56,57,58]. But today WPATH *enforces* normative social transition (to the degree the practitioner sees fit) on individuals who need medical transition (in particular SRS and other genital surgeries) by simply making social transition and a documented 'full time'

[A] *Self-orchiectomies have been documented throughout time. But this isn't an issue of the past. While providing community support I have come across a number of individuals who either had self-orchiectomized, or later decided to do so. While these individuals represent a minority, they are by far not exceptional.*

life in the 'opposite gender' for a minimum of one year an absolute condition for medical treatment[79,80]. The SOC also enforces medical normativity by denying individuals access to SRS only, without prior hormonal treatment[A] or a permanent normative social transition[79,80]. Very different concerns are salient to and systemic oppression is experienced and interpreted very differently. Ultimately, the majority of trans populations are denied the freedom of choice and a true self-expression.

2.2.2 *Gender In The Service Of Heteronormativity*

By the time Benjamin published *The Transsexual Phenomenon* (1966) any reference to hormonal needs had been removed, and by the 1980's Freund et al.'s new classification of "two types of cross-gender identity", homosexual and heterosexual transsexuals[28], was standard practice[1]. This categorization was politically opportunistic and factually irrelevant. Practitioners played on homophobic fears, promoting gender-transition as a means to 'save people from being homosexuals'. By changing an individual's anatomical sexual characteristics the person could be 'turned from a homosexual man into a heterosexual woman'[B].

Such arguments may have been deemed important by professionals to gain social support for sex reassignment, but they also led to a distinct preference to treat people who would, after transition, *be perceived socially as heterosexuals*. This obviously disadvantaged individuals with a homosexual or bisexual sexual orientation[C][56]. This linkage between sexual orientation and gender affiliation remains emotionally and socially very destructive in that it transposes the idea of heteronormativity onto transgender communities (including treatment), and establishes a preference for acceptance and treatment that is unrelated to the need of the individual. The American Psychiatric Association still sees a need to establish this criterion. Today the inclusion of sexual orientation is still mandated as a part of any diagnosis of GID by virtue of the DSM[2].

[A] *With the exception of individuals for whom hormonal treatment is documented to be medically dangerous.*

[B] *At the time only female to male transsexuals were accepted. Individuals furthermore had to state that they were sexually only attracted to males. This, according to the then prevailing nomenclature, was termed 'a homosexual transsexual': medical professionals saw a biological male (a transwoman) who was attracted to a male and concluded that this must be of a homosexual nature (a male attracted to males). They then concluded that 'making a female out of the transsexual' would rid the world of one, potentially even two homosexuals (her partner). Consequently, providing SRS was seen as the lesser of two evils - providing this surgery, or having to look at one more homosexual.*

[C] *In Freund's view a 'homosexual transsexual' is an individual who is typically male and is attracted to males. After gender transition this individual would of course be visibly and, if she had SRS, anatomically female, but Freund's interpretation of this woman's sexual attraction towards men would still be that of a homosexual relationship.*

Meanwhile, Blanchard and later Lawrence, herself co-author and member of the SOC-V6 committee[79], promoted a slightly different interpretation, positioning transsexuality as an expression of auto-erotic fantasies, called autogynephilia[A][6,43]. This theory is probably the one best known by members of the public as it has been widely circulated in popular science magazines such as Scientific American[5].

Ekins sums this up when he writes that in "the tensions between science, politics and clinical intervention"[20] Benjamin had to adapt. "There is evidence to suggest that the logic of 'treatment' and 'politics' (the art of the possible) did, indeed, lead to the compromise of his 'science'"[20]. Ekins also concludes that this led "inevitably to a privileging of a certain sort of transsexual experience and outcome at the expense of other kinds"[20].

Controlling transsexuals, through criteria such as being heterosexual (after transition), maximum passing (through additional surgery) and never publicly disclosing transsexuality, had become more important than the well-being and self-realization of individuals[58]. In a direct parallel to this shift, theoreticians blurred the complexities in trans communities. Elliot states: "in annexing transsexuals to the category of transgender, which is praised for its opposition to sex/gender congruence, Butler and others render aspects of a specifically transsexual experience invisible"[20]. Lombardi concurs, stating that such imposed identities "preclude any attempt at examining the variations found among gender variant populations"[46].

[A] *More recently, the term autoandrophilia has been introduced to offer a 'male equivalent', even though the original theory specifically excluded female born individuals from its scope.*

2.3 The Standards Of Care

The medical treatment of transsexuals is regulated by the *Standards of Care*[79,80] [SOC] of the *World Professional Association for Transgender Health*[79,80] [WPATH]. Most service providers in Canada use Version 6[79], some use Version 7[80]. The SOC is de-facto mandated onto licensed practitioners, and thus indirectly onto any patient who seeks either hormonal treatment [HRT], which requires prescriptions, or surgical interventions, in particular genital surgery [SRS], for which the SOC mandates psychiatric approval and referral.

Unlike other medical standards of care which generally describe *how to factually diagnose and how to treat* patients, the SOC exclusively concerns itself with *who is socially deemed to merit treatment, according to the personal beliefs of the authors*. In fact, the SOC clearly states that, in spite of its existence as a 'medical standard' for over 50 years, "to date, no controlled clinical trials of any [...] hormone regimen have been conducted"[80]. As a result, widely varying treatments are used as individual practitioners or treatment centres make them up at their discretion[80].

The SOC establishes a distinctly pathological view of self-experiences and self-expressions that are outside of what the authors define as normative and thus acceptable. According to the SOC, medical interventions may be justified for individuals the SOC refers to as *"gender nonconforming people"*[80]. But to even be considered, one needs a diagnosis of 'severe GID', the definition of which is entirely left to the American Psychiatric Association [APA] and their Diagnostic and Statistical Manual of Mental Disorders, the DSM[2]. (For details and a definition, see Appendix A.3, *The DSM's Gender Identity Disorder*). According to the authors of the SOC and the DSM, no other reasons, motivations or needs other than their 'disorderly gender identification' can ever exist. For those who are diagnosed with GID, any treatment is granted on the grounds that *hormonal treatment or surgery of the genitals are seen as a suitable intervention to treat an illness of the mind.*

Based on this perspective, the SOC establishes a distinctly one-dimensional interpretation of trans treatment - to induce physical changes in the body so that an individual will socially conform to the more acceptable gender. The 120 page document[80] doesn't even mention that individuals may seek treatment for the emotional benefits of HRT or SRS. The fact that there are individuals who seek treatment for spiritual reasons is also missing entirely.

In typical doublespeak both WPATH[79,80] and some feminist/queer theorists highlight the depressive potential of HRT and position trans treatment solely as a technology to obtain physical changes that are obtained at the cost of these negative emotional experiences[32,67,79,80]. They then require transsexuals to state that HRT is a thoroughly positive emotional experience[79,80], or scold people for using medical technology for the (sole) purpose of normative compliance[10,32,33,67]. This doublespeak demonizes and erases the complexities found in trans communities.

2.3.1 *Putting The Standards Of Care Into Context*

While the SOC plays a major role in defining the lives of many trans people, it is important to recognize that there are significant differences in how medical treatment is provided to trans people around the world. The authors of the SOC may claim that they are "a world professional organization"[79,80], but in reality the SOC is only mandated onto people seeking trans treatment in a Western European context, most notably in Western Europe, North and South America, Australia and a few other places around the globe that have been influenced by European and American colonization. Two complex examples include professional applications in places such as Thailand and Iran. In both countries the SOC is applied to foreigners seeking SRS but not to local trans populations.

Often it is argued that the SOC and psycho-pathologization of trans people are needed in order to provide access to insurance coverage for trans-related medical interventions. While this assumption is questionable in and of itself, it must be recognized that the treatments covered by insurance vary greatly. For example, some countries mandate that facial hair removal for female to male trans people must be covered by insurance. In these countries, trans people will have to qualify for this intervention through a local reinterpretation of the SOC. As hair removal is not generally regulated, everybody who can pay for the procedure themselves can obtain it at their discretion. In these places the SOC acts not only as a gateway for treatment, but also as a an instrument of repressive social control of people who do not have the means to pay out of pocket.

Geographic differences also create differences in legal interpretations. For example, some countries require trans people to undergo SRS, or at least sterilization, in order to have their gender legally recognized. In other places, such a recognition is an administrative change that does not require surgical interventions. Consequently, in some countries the SOC is used indirectly to regulate access to legal recognition, while in others it is not. Through this conflation of medical and legal issues, many trans people feel forced to undergo surgical procedures they may not have wanted in order to obtain legal recognition, while at the same time the SOC acts as a delay to obtain such recognition.

No matter where one lives, various treatment centres and individual medical practitioners may use different interpretations of the SOC, in particular when it comes to accessing 'restricted treatments', such as HRT, breast surgery, and SRS. While everybody adheres to minimum waiting times, some treatment centres interpret the SOC as allowing HRT and breast reduction surgeries before the 'real life test', while others require the 'real life test' before allowing any of these interventions.

In Ontario, Canada where my study was conducted, all medical trans treatment is controlled by the SOC. However, there are differences in interpretation between treatment centres, in particular when it comes to HRT. Currently in Ontario, only one treatment centre, the Centre for Addictions and Mental Health (CAMH), can offer health-insurance-covered SRS. Consequently, their interpretation of the SOC carries significant importance for all trans people who seek SRS and cannot afford to pay for it themselves. Again, the financial means of trans people are used as leverage to enforce a specific interpretation of the SOC, and of their lives, within a specific geographic zone.

2.3.2 *The Euro-Western Pathological Approach*

Transsexuality is exclusively self-identified. Even the DSM[2] notes this. Consequently, no external diagnosis through observation or tests is possible. But can a transsexual 'just be trusted' in their self-identification? Apparently, the authors of the SOC feel that *stating one's self-identification is not a sufficient criteria for treatment.* Instead, the SOC creates and mandates completely arbitrary and unrelated but 'verifiable' hoops as substitutes for scientific diagnostic criteria. This includes an arbitrary timeline ('waiting times' typically totalling 2-6 years for SRS[56]), an arbitrary mandated order of health care interventions (psychotherapy, then HRT, then SRS), and prescribed lifestyle interventions (both normative cross-gender living and mandated sexual behaviour for a minimum of one year)[79,80]. Only then can SRS even be considered. The SOC, version 6, also mandates a prescribed employment status, thereby excluding retired and unemployed individuals as well as people with disabilities from access to any medical trans treatment[79]. Meanwhile, the SOC explicitly bans some self-expressions. For example SRS (or an orchiectomy) cannot be allowed without a clinically verified permanent (1 year minimum) social transition, even if the individual does not wish to transition socially[79,80]. Some other highlights the SOC gives no consideration to include:

▶ if the individual actually desires any of these mandated measures

▶ if some of the conditions, in particular the enforced cross-living, may be inherently dangerous in the individual's social setting

▶ if the order 'cross living, *then* surgery' (instead of 'surgery, *then* cross living', or surgery only) is in fact meaningful and the best treatment for everybody

▶ that, for some trans men, cross-living is virtually impossible before they can obtain a mastectomy

▶ if the normative social transition psychiatry prescribes is a true self-expression of each and every individual (see 6.2, *Our Bodies, Our Sex - It's More Complex*; 7.2.1, *'Transition' And 'Passing' In The Fluid Group*).

In such a dictatorial set-up many invent a new life in the medical office[14,56]. It starts with stating that HRT is a positive experience. While this is true for many, some experience no noticeable or a distinctly negative effect from HRT. Individuals claim that their motivation for treatment is normative body modifications as this is all the SOC allows[79,80]. The need for such lies deprive people from obtaining the best possible care, or any care for experiences they cannot mention. This can lead to a complete denial of access to primary health care. Meanwhile, practitioners have a reinforced view of trans communities (and the needs of individuals) that in fact is not real, but is solely constructed for the benefit of the medical practitioner[14,56,61].

When these practitioners then draw-up the next iteration of the SOC, they are prone to base their writing on reinforced lies and pretended lifestyles, rather than the real needs and desired self-expressions of trans people. Throughout the history of the SOC[79,80] and applicable DSM[2] sections on GID and transvestic fetishism, subsequent iterations allowed more people treatment (e.g. trans men, homosexual and bisexual individuals), but were more narrow in their prescriptiveness of what amounts to a European, white and highly sexist interpretation of gender, gender roles and gender expressions steeped in a binary interpretation of gender and sexuality. This may not be intentional, but two effects combine to create this result:

▶ In the 1950's a set of earrings and long hair pretty much designated an individual as female. Pants or a suit were indicative of a male, at least in Western, European cultures. Over time, many of these social markers have lost their gender specificity and while I applaud the freedom of expression gained through the dismantling of such stereotyping, this leaves trans people with fewer and fewer social markers to 'prove' that they live a specific stereotypical gender role. To compensate, both expectations of practitioners and expressions of individuals have over time shifted from more cultural to physical, and therefore often more overtly sexualized gender markers.

▶ According to the SOC[79,80] the 'lived gender' must be verified and approved by a practitioner licensed to diagnose GID, usually a psychiatrist. In North America most psychiatrists are white, male and upper middle-class. California reported in 2004 that more than two thirds of practicing psychiatrists were white and an even higher ratio were male[45]. This can introduce a cultural bias into the already highly subjective process of 'diagnosing lived gender', in particular if the cultural expression of gender is not familiar to the practitioner. Individuals from minorities will react to such expectations by adapting to limited Western gender expressions, or may find themselves excluded from treatment.

Foucault noted in 1988 that over time the institutionalized knowledge of medicine invaded more and more of everyday life[27]. Such knowledge is by far not neutral. The colonization of transsexual self-expressions by physicians enforcing an ever stricter regime of social morality - of behavioural and physical 'appropriateness' - continues to limit self-expressions and self-experiences along normative expectations. Today, the SOC constructs any self-experience of transsexuality as a pathology, assigned by physicians at their sole discretion, clearly stating that the means to physically express transsexuality through one's body "is not a right that must be granted upon request"[79].

As a post-trans individual, I ask myself where in this scenario can we find people whose consideration includes our self-identifications, our self-determination, our self-actualization, our self-realization and our humanity?

2.4 The Privilege Of Being 'Properly' Gendered

This section touches upon the costs of failing at gender normativity. In western society trans people are marginalized. Or, to put this differently, individuals who are *'properly' gendered*, according to social expectations, are extended one of the most fundamental privileges this society has to offer: *the privilege of genderedness*. According to Mandlis, loosing the privilege of genderedness leads to "[the] exclusion from the category 'human'"[48].

The consequences of not being consistently normatively gendered range from involuntary medical interventions to psycho-pathologization, social ostracism and a legal status with formal rather than substantive rights[40,48,50,56]A. A ruling of the US Seventh Circuit Court in *Ulane v. Eastern Airlines Inc.* exemplifies this. In a still widely quoted precedent, the court found that the plaintiff, Karen Ulane, a 'pre-op transwoman', is not protected under the *Civil Rights Act* because the Civil Rights Act only applies to men and women, but not to 'other and undefined people'[44].

Many jurisdictions, including province of Ontario, have recently updated their human rights legislation to include 'gender expression' and 'gender identity' as prohibited grounds for discrimination. The term *gender expression* is reasonably clear. It encompasses dressing, appearance and behaviour. The term 'gender identity' may be more contestable. The problem of course is that *gender identity* is not a visible identification (such as being a member of a visible minority), but a self-identification. The legal system usually does not accept self-identifications. To the legal system one is not 'John Doe' because one says so, but because *one's documentation* says so. It remains to be seen if *gender identity* will actually be interpreted as a *gender self-identification* (which, in my opinion, the text of the law should state), or if it is an identification that can be challenged and is ultimately assigned by an expert, such as a psychiatrist. To date, no legal precedent exists in Ontario, so only time will tell what legal practice will emerge.

Such laws only solve certain legal aspects of trans people's lives, and even so, only after the trans person goes to court, which usually requires a substantial amount of funding. Furthermore, if a trans person chooses to go to court, then this act alone will 'out' the individual as trans to any involved parties, as well as to the

---

[A] *'Formal' rights are rights that are extended to an individual on paper, but the individual has limited or no ability to claim or enforce if these are infringed upon. Substantive rights are rights that can be enforced through procedural, legal and judicial means. Formal rights are often disregarded because it is known that they cannot be enforced.*

public and the media due of the public nature of court proceedings. This alone presents a significant challenge and disadvantages trans people, no matter if they can then expect a fair trial or not. *Ulane v. Eastern Airlines Inc.* is ample proof that this is by no means guaranteed[50].

Most importantly, discrimination, oppression and societal expectations, as well as feelings about trans people and trans communities, are not changed by adding a law. Neither are medical attitudes and practices. Having a right on paper does not automatically mean that one can exercise this right, and being legally protected does not mean that trans people will not continue to be subject to slander, humiliation, assault, rape, and murder - all of which have been illegal before the above human rights legislation was enacted.

Ultimately for many, SRS is the one intervention with the promise to 'fix' most of the above. In current legal interpretations, SRS certainly does improve the legal position of one's claim to a specific place in the gender binary. Other improvements meanwhile, such as social acceptance, are far more complex and vary greatly by individual and by situation. For one, the quality of the result of women's SRS are considered to be far better than these for men, usually allowing full intimate and sexual integration, while the results of male surgery may not always allow 'passing in the change-room' and at this time offers only limited sexual functionality.

Within the constructs of the SOC, SRS is seen as a completion and ultimate commitment within the gender binary. As such, it comes with the expectation of social recognition of one's gender, but this assumption is largely flawed. After all, how often do we judge each other by the looks of our primary genitals *in a social context?* Social 'passing', or acceptance, does not come from genitals. It comes from looks of visible body features, one's presentation, behaviour and, probably most importantly, from one's self-assertiveness. Ultimately, individual experiences depend much more on how people integrate being trans into their lives, and how comfortable they are with themselves and their self-expression, rather than on how stereotypical an individual is perceived within the gender binary.

Nevertheless, SRS does allow some people to use social spaces where nudity is required (such as saunas or change rooms), it permits them to use emergency medical services with much less fear of mistreatment, abuse or denial of service. It allows people to get care in nursing and retirement homes (see 2.2, *From History To Status Quo*), at least when it comes to being assigned to the gender appropriate ward. While this is a clear improvement, trans people remain highly vulnerable in such settings in particular when it comes to access to hormonal treatment. Even though often overstated, the legal, medical and social benefits of SRS are tangible and can significantly reduce social fears. The question of course remains if an individual should have to obtain SRS at all to get social, medical and legal benefits, or if this decision should rather relate to concerns of self-experience, body-image, sexual functioning and sexual integration. This still does not address either transphobia or lack of knowledge by service providers in various settings.

Additional pressure is created through the normative ideology of the SOC and the medical model, and indirectly through the SOC's Catch-22 mandate of psychological therapy, which can also reinforce normative models. For many, peer pressure to 'pass' from within trans communities is also an important personal complication.

All the above legal, social, structural, administrative, peer-related, medical and therapeutic frameworks simultaneously put a lot of pressure onto individuals[39,48]. Not being 'properly gendered' means to fail within each and every one of these frameworks. If this means potentially loosing any and all rights to access systems and services, existential fears can develop, in particular when it comes to the fear of denial of medical care, or of protection from violence. Within such networks of power-relations and gate keeping, any claims that transsexuals have 'true free choices' and that their lives are 'true reflections of self-identifications' becomes naïve at best and annihilating at worst.

To then accuse transsexuals of manufacturing "their narrative in a fashion that will facilitate access to technology after having researched the medical literature to ensure the 'correctness' of their narrative (Butler, 2004; Namaste, 2000; Prosser, 1998)"[48] and *'choosing'* SRS without a 'recognized *medical* need' (which, for some critics, *never* exists), not only ignores all the social ramifications and the practical implications the privilege of being gendered bestows, but, on a more practical level, is equivalent to asking transsexuals to take any and all ostracisms and abuses these systems offer, while never taking advantage of their knowledge of how these systems really work.

In typical doublespeak both WPATH[79,80] and some feminist/queer theorists highlight the depressive potential of HRT and position trans treatment solely as a technology to obtain physical changes that are obtained at the cost of these negative emotional experiences[32,67,79,80]. They then require transsexuals to state that HRT is a thoroughly positive emotional experience[79,80], or scold people for using medical technology for the (sole) purpose of normative compliance[10,32,33,67]. This doublespeak demonizes and erases the complexities found in trans communities.

2.5 Social Theories - Not Quite There Yet

Several social theories, queer theories and many feminisms in particular, have made attempts to be inclusive of trans people. Sadly, they have yet to fully accept the complexities of difference that trans individuals present. This is surprising. After all, embracing difference is at the core of queer theory, and anti-oppressiveness is a fundamental principle of feminism.

Some second wave feminists[A] have positioned transsexuality as completely unacceptable. For example Raymond's essentialist interpretation of womanhood and gender in 1979, and her subsequent vilification of transsexual women[67], is a reprise of the pre-1980's medical view that transwomen are 'very serious male fetishists'[4], and of the just emerging idea that transsexuality is an 'auto-erotic paraphilia'[43]. In this context (female) trans people were called *creations of medical technology, frauds, deranged males, dilettantes* or *recreationalists*[31,32,67]. The existence of transmen was simply erased in her critique.

Many of these theories were based on the pre-1970's medical view that all trans-sexuals (transwomen) are men exclusively sexually attracted to other men. They were medically classified as 'male homosexuals'[4,6,28, 54] based on their birth-sex designations. Medical practitioners insisted that transwomen remain classified as male for life. Any sexual activity between a transwoman and a male was classified as a male homosexual act, even after SRS. Medical and social transition was seen as 'a superficial cure for homosexuality'. After treatment, the individual would no longer be 'visibly homosexual' and thus could 'socially pass as a heterosexual'. Nonetheless, for both the aforementioned feminist theorists and medical profession-als, it appeared utterly impossible that a transwoman could in fact be a woman.

The idea that the presence or absence of a penis at birth is the sole marker of gender has been largely dismissed in third wave feminism and recent queer theory. However, while trans people have become 'acceptable' within these theories, the interpretation of transsexuality as a mental illness still prevails. Instead of accepting the full range of mental, physical and spiritual complexities and individual expres-

---

[A] *Within a North American context, feminism is generally defined in partly overlapping 'waves': first wave (before 1960), second wave (from 1960 to 1980), and third wave (after 1990). First wave feminism is a re-naming of the women's rights movement. Second wave feminism is the women's liberation movement with a very essentialist, biology oriented definition of womanhood. It was heavily criticized for being biased towards white, European/North-American Christian culture. Third wave feminism tried to address this criticism by integrating elements of anti-oppressive theory, anti-racism theory, queer theory and several other theories, while offering a more post-modernist interpreta-tion of womanhood.*

sions, including that transwomen can be women, womanhood is recast from a restrictive 2 point binary (female and male) to an only slightly more complex binary-based continuum (female, male, and 'everyone in between'). This is then said to be inclusive of everybody. But as Elliot points out, to place transwomen on a continuum of women where some are pure women and others are "some hybrid mix" is hardly inclusive[21]. As a mathematically inclined scientist it is my interpretation that adding any number of 'continua', or dimensions, will not create a full understanding of the complexities of trans people as there will always be another dimension that has not been identified. Therefore, only self-identification and self-determination without external labelling can ever be an acceptable theoretical framework. Clearly, the existing theoretical interpretations of the lives of trans people are problematic in many ways.

From trans perspectives, any theorist who feels entitled to define gender has to address three fundamental questions: what is gender, how is it acquired, and who is entitled to assign a specific gender to any individual. After these questions have been answered within a specific theoretical framework, theorists are supposed to respect their own definitions. If they do not, then their interpretations become inconsistent, and their positions are no longer founded in their respective theoretical frameworks. Let's start with the first question.

What is gender? As opposed to the individual complexities found in my study, theoreticians often define gender as based in, or independent of anatomy. But either definition is problematic. If gender is defined as based in anatomy, then it is nothing but another term for a person's sex. If a theory defines gender as an independent personality trait, then it becomes absurd to single out trans people for exhibiting a gender that 'does not match' their anatomical sexuality. This is a fundamental fallacy in feminism, queer theory and the medical/psychiatric model of trans lives. For example, psychiatry claims that gender is a solely self-identified and independent personality trait of individuals[1,2]. Next, medical professionals declare, through the SOC[79,80], that the lives of trans people need to be regulated, policed, and externally approved. This prompts an important question. Is gender really acknowledged as independent within a theoretical model, if its expression is curtailed just as soon as it does not meet strict, binary expectations? Ultimately, none of the above theories can offer a definition of 'gender' that is not inherently self-contradictory.[A]

The next fundamental question is about how gender is acquired. Gender can be either cultural and learned, or it can be a mixture of biological predisposition and

---

[A] *For a further theoretical discussion see my upcoming publication* "Why We Don't Exist: Colonized Bodies, Colonized Minds, Erased Lives - Challenging the Imperialistic Dogma Of 'The Common Transsexual'"[60]

cultural learning. Gender cannot be exclusively biological because at least gender-expression is highly culturally determined. Many queer theorists, such as Butler, insist that gender is exclusively social[10]. In this scenario, being trans - if it is not unquestionably accepted - must therefore be interpreted as 'some form of a learning disorder'. Trans people 'do not learn their gender correctly'. This would put any expression of being trans into the realm of a mental illness, but it would also, even though unarticulated, surmise that there is in fact 'a correct gender to be learned'. That 'correct gender' is, once again, the one derived from sexual anatomy. This prompts another important question. If queer theory states that all self-identifications and self-expressions are equally valid and valued, then why are some expressions, particularly these of trans people who seek medical transition, so heavily criticized by some queer theorists? Butler, for example, states that decisions on trans treatment should be made by psychiatrists[10]. In other words, she argues that any form of medical trans treatment must be a third-party moral judgment and cannot be a free self-determination. Isn't this eerily reminiscent of Orwell's *Animal Farm,* where "all animals are equal, but some are more equal than others"[65]? Some people are entitled to self-determination, but some are not?

The third fundamental question is about who is entitled to assign gender. Two answers are possible: the individual, or some external, socially designated 'expert'. The medical community favours external 'expertise' - their own. Medical professionals not only make-up the parameters according to which sex is assigned, they also assign individual labels, surgically conform newborns to their expectations, and go on to declare individuals who do not agree with their 'expert findings' as mentally ill. There is no recourse for the individual, and no alternative way to obtain treatment, as this too is entirely controlled by medical practitioners.

Based on their principles, feminists should locate a clear power imbalance in this set-up. They should interpret the medical profession's privilege to unilaterally define and assign sex as paternalistic. Feminists should further point out that at the time medical sexing was instituted and later legally mandated (from about 1850 to 1930), it was an expression of male privilege, taking away rights from female service providers such as midwives in favour of physicians who were almost exclusively male. Feminists will recognize that such paternalistically forced sexing in the name of the government upholds patriarchy. This official act of: designating - or manufacturing - acceptable penises and vaginae, bestowing privilege on people with such 'acceptable penises', and creating an assumption of femininity and masculinity based on anatomy, not only perpetuates the oppression of a variety of women, but also of human gender complexity in general.

The aforementioned interpretation of trans people[31,32,67], and of many others who adhere to the doctrine 'womyn born womyn', prompt another important question. How can it be that *some* feminists vehemently oppose patriarchy, expose male privilege and the oppression of women, but are so very eager to accept the verdict (that transwomen are not really women and transmen can only be women) rendered by such a male dominated, patriarchal power-structure? Is it because the verdict supports their fears, their transphobia, and their attempts to monopolize women's oppression? Whatever the case, this supports the patriarchal exclusion, vilification and demonization of transwomen, let alone transmen and others.

If gender were assumed to be both social and biological, then a set of very simple explanations could be hypothesized to explain a number of expressions of being trans. However, this explanation would be difficult to accommodate in queer theory as well as in feminism because of the biological component assigned to gender. It would also be impossible to incorporate into the medical model because of the component of self-determination within the social realm of gender. From time to time scientists claim that they have found 'a physical cause of transsexuality'. However, ultimately it is irrelevant why people are trans, as long as their self-expressions and self-identifications are not artificially curtailed by social theories or medical practices that arbitrarily imply such 'cause'. What is relevant is that trans people's self-identifications and their self-determinations are honoured, and that they are allowed to self-realize their full potential freely. My survey results showed that a wide range of self-identifications exists, by far surpassing the limitations of any of the current theoretical interpretations (see 5.3, Self-Awareness; 6.3, Beyond The 'Cross-Gender' Diagnosis; 7.2, Troubles With 'Transition').

As a mathematically inclined scientist, in order to acknowledge this diversity within social and medical theory, let alone practice, it is necessary to allow for an *unlimited* complexity of self-identifications (and self-realizations). The choice of a fractal for the cover of this book is an artistic representation of such unlimited complexity. Within social theories this means that adding diversity one marginalized group after another, or 'one trans community after another', will never yield an all-inclusive theory of humanity, nor of trans people. The only way to include *everybody,* mathematically speaking, is by using a zero-dimensional explanation and relate to people not as groups, nor in any other way as designated as something, but as single individuals, leaving self-identifications and self-expressions to people, instead of to theorists, or to moral judges. Of course today's society is far from accepting people's self-identifications in relation to gender and sexuality without any moral judgment.

In the last edition of the SOC, various feminists and queer theorists are quoted in support of the SOC's authors belief that being trans is exclusively social[8,24,73,80]. This is used to place all trans-related medical treatment decisions into the domain of psychiatry[80]. To maintain this status quo, it appears that the aforementioned theorists, and the authors of the SOC, define trans people based on a belief that the self-expressions they currently see represent the entirety of trans people. This belief guarantees that no fundamental rethinking of theories or transformation of services is needed. But as long as trans people must conform to theoretical and treatment expectations, trans communities continue to be created artificially instead of becoming an expression of lived self-realization. Ultimately, it is the belief that all trans people must, somehow, fit into existing social theories, and that a 'standardized trans person' can be defined for the purpose of providing medical treatment, that is the root cause of systemic limitations of trans people's lives.

I am not asking people to change their beliefs. But I am asking people to acknowledge that their philosophical positions are *beliefs,* not facts. I also ask people to respect that every individual is entitled to hold their own beliefs, even if these are different from expectations. I ask everybody to respect that this includes the right to express any belief through one's thoughts, one's body, one's values, one's self-identifications and one's self-expressions. However, it does not include a right to force one's beliefs onto others by means of coercion, threat, or violence.

Sadly, this society is still far away from recognizing such basic truths universally. The following example illustrates this very well. In 2012 *any* therapy designed to change a person's *sexual orientation* (presumably from homosexual to heterosexual) was made illegal by the California Legislature[11]. This made California the first jurisdiction worldwide to enact such a law. The same law also prohibits psychological treatment to change a person's gender self-perception or self-interpretation. But there is a snag. The law leaves a loophole that allows individuals who are licensed to practice medicine to continue to apply treatments to try to change an individual's gender self-identification. It specifically states that the ban on 'gender self-identification reversal therapy' only applies to practitioners who are legally regulated as psychologists or psychotherapists, but it does not include psychiatrists[11].

Ultimately, trans people are still not entitled to hold and express their beliefs freely, to live their self-identifications without a threat of 'corrective' violence. But the truly sad part is not that such violence as 'gender reversal therapy' is legal everywhere, but rather that in spite of all the wonderful theories about acceptance and anti-oppressiveness, a large number of people who claim to uphold such beliefs choose to remain silent. Some even choose to actively oppress trans people.

Chapter 2: How We Got To Where We Are

Contents

▶ A short history of trans-identifications and treatment by the medical system

▶ The creation of the Standards of Care [SOC] for treatment (2.2)

▶ An examination of the privilege of bring 'properly' gendered in a gendered world (2.4)

▶ An exploration of the interpretation of trans people in social theories, and their respective influence on, and expectations of trans lives (2.5)

Conclusions

▶ There is a professional conflict between the interpretation of trans-sexuality as physical (with HRT and SRS as a solution), or as mental (with psychiatric treatment as a solution).

▶ Over the past 100 years, the interpretation of trans people has shifted from a life-expression to a psycho-pathology.

▶ Today's medical standards of care for treatment [SOC] are a reflection of cultural and social normativity - a tool to use the power of the medical system to impose the gender binary onto trans people.

▶ The SOC uses a 'one fits all' approach which, according to its authors, is sufficient to cover all needs trans people may have.

▶ Some assumptions of social theories and the medical interpretation of transsexuality as a mental issue self-reinforce.

▶ Professionals and theoreticians create their own truth by ignoring the full complexity and diversity within trans communities.

▶ The full range of diversity and the full human complexity relating to gender and sexuality can only be honoured if individuals are not limited by theoretical or treatment expectations. Only self-determination and free self-realization without predefined expectations will truly liberate trans people (and others).

3

COMPARING

DATA

3.1 *For The Purpose Of Comparing Research*

As mentioned before (see 1.1, *A Question Yet To Be Answered*; 1.1.2, *Participants*), it is important for my research to ascertain that clinical researchers should have seen the diversity I am documenting. (Statistically, they also should have invited representatives of all the self-interpretations and self-expressions found in my research). Establishing this is done in 3 steps:

▶ Only participants who would qualify to participate in 'trans research' even under the most stringent interpretations of the term 'trans' were invited (see 1.1.2, *Participants*). This means that individuals must have had some form of contact with the medical system.

▶ These participation criteria were verified through questions in the survey. Participants who did not report that they meet the participation criteria would have been excluded. (Note: no participants needed to be excluded during this verification process).

▶ Quantitative statistical data was collected during the survey in order to make a comparison with other surveys on trans populations possible. This allowed for a confirmation that the populations queried were indeed similar.

This last position is problematic in that it required me to use questions and provide answer choices that are comparable to existing research, even though I may not agree with the line of questioning, the predefined answers, or the language used. Nevertheless, this was necessary to establish comparability.

It is important to recognize this, and to push for change in any future research on trans communities. I recognize that offering 12 choices[A] for 'gender identity' makes the process of analyzing data far more efficient than asking participants to state their gender self-identification in their own words, without providing predefined cookie-cutter labels. I also recognize that within the complexity of trans communities, such predefined answers may be leading, interpreted as discriminatory, or even worthless. Most importantly, the meaning of many of the terms used varies greatly within trans communities. While this still allows for comparisons to other surveys (as these

---

[A] *The choices in the survey offered were, similar to TransPulse[76]: 'Woman or Girl', 'Man or Boy', 'MtF', 'FtM', 'TransWoman (or Girl)', 'TransMan (or Boy)', 'Two Spirit', 'Intersex', 'Genderqueer', 'Bi-Gender', "Not sure or questioning" and 'Other, please specify'. Participants were asked to check any combination that applied to them.*

suffer from the same problems), it becomes highly questionable how useful the responses will in fact be.

Some of the terms used in clinical surveys can be directly degrading, abusive or misinterpreting of some people or all trans communities (even if these are used within trans communities themselves). For example, the term *'felt gender'* implies that this 'felt' gender comes in contrast to something else, presumably to *'real gender'?* A transsexual person does not have *'a felt gender',* distinct from that person's 'real gender'. A transsexual person has, like everybody else, *a gender.* *'Passing as one's gender'* or even *'passable as one's gender'* is another example. It implies some form of deceit. A designation such as *'being recognized as one's gender'* would be preferable. However, if my research would use this more neutral and accepting language, critics would rightly point out that I asked a different question, and therefore responses are not comparable.

For the reasons mentioned above, it is difficult for this small research project to introduce new language and ranges of predefined choices that are more community friendly and community responsive. But the hope remains that large surveys on trans communities will be designed differently in the future, led by trans community researchers and a sensitivity to trans communities, instead of propagating outdated, derogatory and limiting lines of questioning.

3.2 *Reporting On Gender Affiliations*

There is one aspect of reporting data in trans surveys I cannot leave unaddressed, even in this small project, as it distorts results so dramatically that, in my opinion, such research becomes largely useless. As stated in 2.3.2 (*The Euro-Western Pathological Approach*), it is problematic to use externally assigned birth-sexes to group trans people for the purpose of reporting shared experiences, in particular as being trans already implies that participants do not accept this type of categorization, or at the very least reject being categorized (see 7.2.1, *'Transition' And 'Passing' In The Fluid Group*). Consequently, I will present individuals according to their reported gender affiliation, not according to birth-sex (or any derivative thereof). Data from participants who checked only female gender affiliations ('woman', 'girl', 'MtF', 'TransWoman',...) are grouped as *the female spectrum* (28 participants or 58%). Data from individuals who checked only male gender affiliations ('man', 'boy', FtM, TransMan',...) are grouped as *the male spectrum* (14 participants or 29%). Data representing participants who chose a non-gendered affiliation or who chose both male and female gender affiliations are grouped as *the fluid spectrum* (6 participants or 13%).

Reported Gender Affiliation[A]

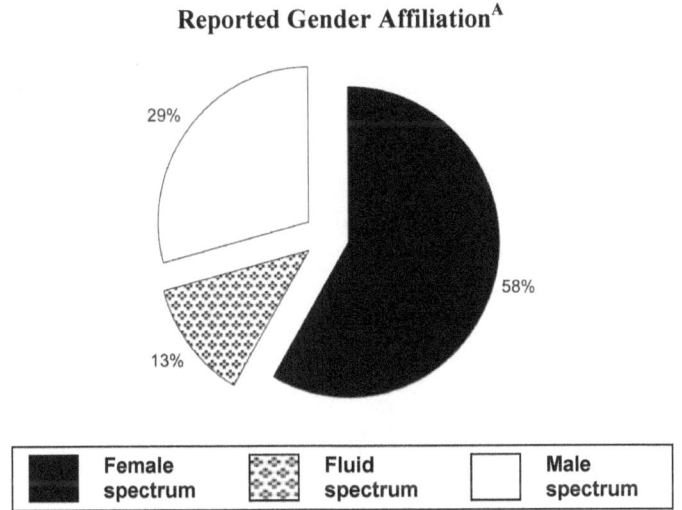

| Female spectrum | Fluid spectrum | Male spectrum |

[A] *Please note: all pie-charts indicate percentages in relation to the total number of participants in the survey, or in relation to the group the diagram represents. For details on charts, please also refer to Appendix A.1, Reading Charts.*

It is probably obvious that individuals who were assigned to the fluid spectrum reported a distribution of assigned birth sexes (65% male, 35% female). However, it is far less obvious that this can also be true for both of the other groups. While in this survey the birth sex indicated by male spectrum participants *happened to be* female for all participants, this was not true for female spectrum participants where the reported birth sexes were 96% male, 4% female. The diagram below shows the reported gender affiliation, indicating birth sex designation.

Reported Gender Affiliation with Subdivision by Birth Sex Designation

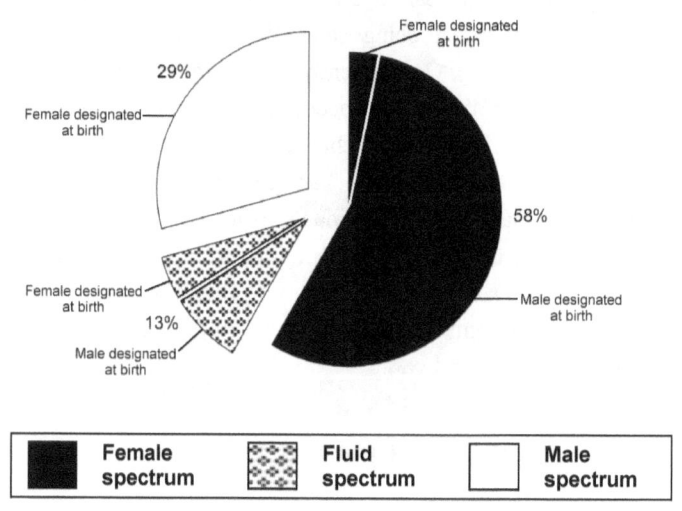

3.3 General Demographic Data

All participants who indicated their place of residence lived in Southern Ontario, with locations including London, Hamilton, Barrie, Toronto, Peterborough, Ottawa and many others. Just over half of participants stated that they lived in the Greater Toronto Area[A] (54%). Few participants lived in small town and rural settings (8%). Such urban preferences of participants have been reported in many other surveys on trans populations, including NTCE & NGLTF (2009)[63,64] and TransPulse (2009)[76].

Of the participants who indicated either a male or female gender affiliation, 65% positioned themselves within the female spectrum, while 35% within the male. This renders the survey clearly female dominated. As such, it is in line with other partly randomized surveys on trans populations. Examples include: Dispenza (2012)[17]; NTCE & NGLTF (2009, 2010)[63,64]; Singh et al. (2011)[72]; TransPulse (2009)[76].

3.3.1 Ethnicity And Racialized Identities

A significant majority of participants described themselves as 'White Canadian, or European' (88%). A few identified as Aboriginal and 'East Asian' (5% each). One participant identified as Middle Eastern and another as Latin American (2% each). Two participants selected multiple ethno-racial backgrounds (5%). These distributions are not representative of the general population, but are similar to what is at this time found in all non ethno-racial specific surveys on trans populations in North America. Examples include: NTCE[63]; TransPulse[76].

The small number of non-white participants does not allow for a statistical analysis of their specific experiences. This is sad as an analysis is long overdue of how Western European cultural and ethnic expectations influence and limit self-expressions and access to trans treatment. I furthermore believe that trans communities as well as treatment providers could benefit greatly from studying non Western European expressions of gender, and non Western European interpretations and social acceptance of 'trans people'.

[A] *Area defined as Postal Codes starting with 'M'*

3.3.2 Age Distribution

Reported ages ranged from 18 years (the minimum to participate) to over 60 years. The average age was 40. This is significantly higher than what large surveys report (NTCE[63]; TransPulse[76]). This high average age is particularly significant in a break-down of reported gender affiliations. The average age of participants in the male spectrum was 33, while it was 37 in the fluid spectrum, but it was 43 in the female spectrum.

While this higher average age may introduce a slight bias in favour of older participants, in particular in the female spectrum, I believe that the data remains comparable to other surveys if this bias is kept in mind when comparing quantitative data. As all age ranges are present, the influence on the qualitative analysis should be minimal. In particular a different age distribution is not an indication that any of the participant experiences should not be present in clinical studies.

Age Distribution, by Gender-Spectrum[A]

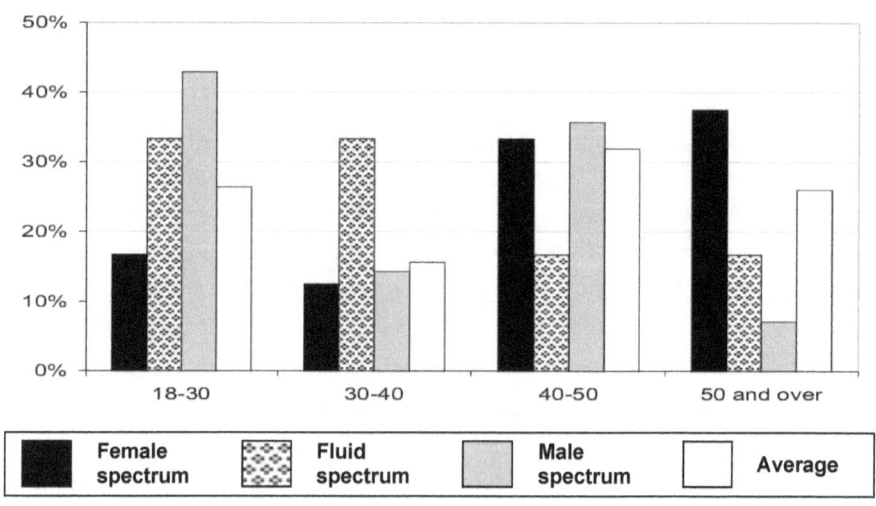

[A] *Reading guide: all bar-charts reporting percentages indicate the percentage of participants in relation to the total number of participants in their gender-spectrum. All averages are weighed by the number of participants in each spectrum For details on charts, please also refer to Appendix A.1, Reading Charts.*

3.3.3 *Education & Employment*

Other surveys have found that while trans populations report a significantly higher than average education, they also report a significantly lower than average income[63,76]. This survey is no exception: 67% of respondents indicated that they either attend college or university or have graduated (54% had graduated, 24% with a graduate or professional degree). However, the types of education were unequally distributed between gender affiliations, with an attendance or graduation rate of 86% in the male spectrum, 50% in the fluid spectrum and 62% in the female spectrum.

Level of Education, by Gender-Spectrum

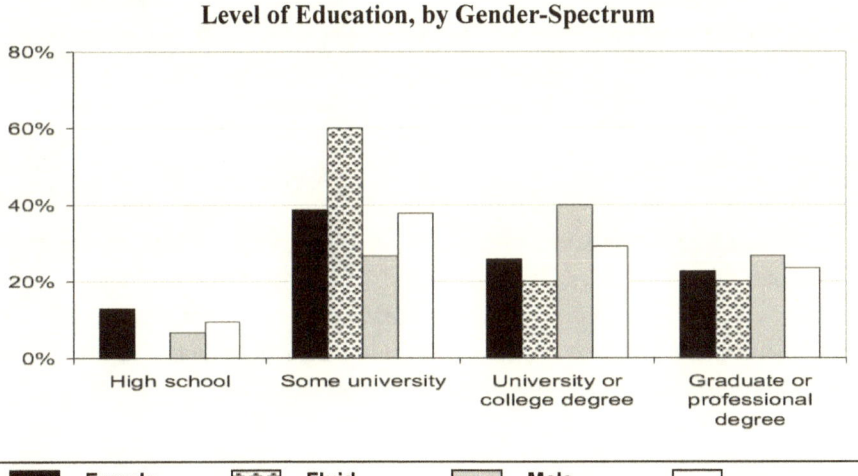

Enrolment in Post-Secondary Educational Institutions, by Gender-Spectrum

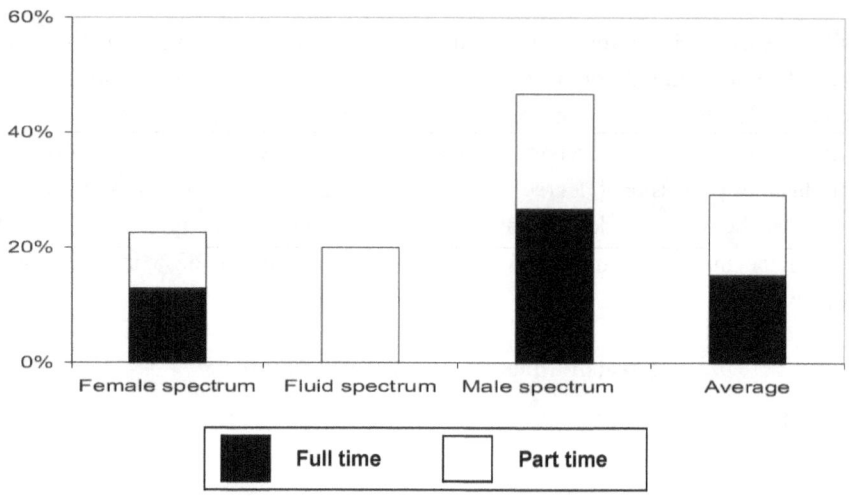

The reported education levels are very much in line with other surveys on trans populations with the exception that fewer female spectrum participants were currently enrolled in school. This can be attributed to the large number of older female participants who are more likely to have their education completed than younger participants and therefore would no longer be enrolled.

3.3.4 Family & Income

Equally comparable to other surveys is the reported structure of incomes and of supported family members. Female spectrum respondents indicated that their income supports an average of 1.9 persons, fluid spectrum participants 1.5 people and male spectrum participants 1.4. Both the NTCE[63] and TransPulse[76] have shown that female spectrum participants support more dependents than male spectrum participants do, just as is the case in society at large.

However, the question 'number of dependent(s) supported' can include any person supported in any way, including an individual abroad, a former spouse or partner after a divorce or separation, or a child that does not live with the trans person. It is therefore much broader than the direct in-home care of children and rather related to financial obligations, reducing the individual's disposable income. Any commitment of time and labour relating to care of children or other people in the lives of trans people, and the related difficulties of coordinating support-tasks and work, is not investigated. At this time we do not even know how many trans people are full- or part-time caregivers of dependents, either as a sole caregivers, or within the framework of a family.

Average Number of Dependents Supported, by Gender-Spectrum

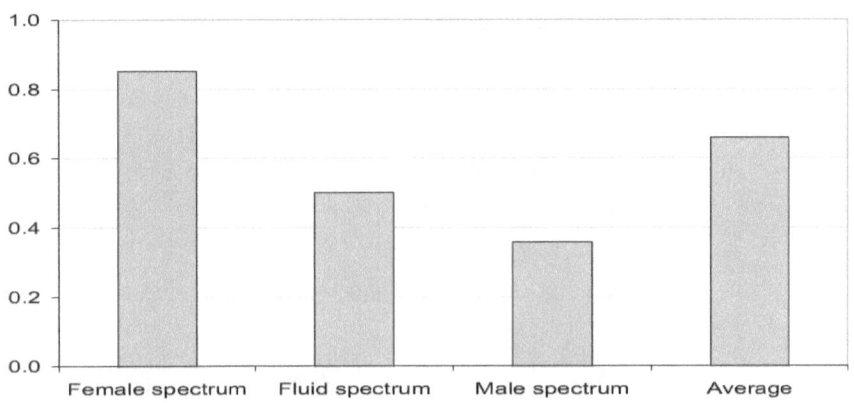

In spite of the aforementioned very high average education levels, the resulting income distribution indicates that a large number of trans individuals and trans families live on an annual disposable income of $15,000 per person or less.

Trans People with a Per Person Income of $15,000 or less, by Gender-Spectrum

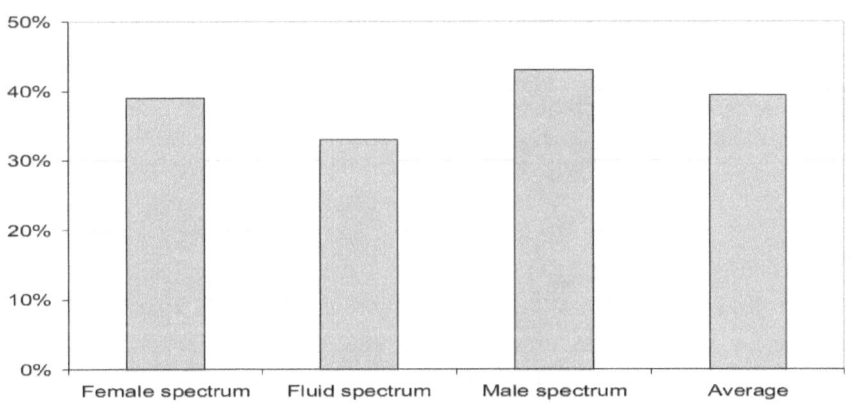

While these numbers are very much in line with older Ontario surveys, such as TransPulse (2009)[76], and thus suggest comparability between survey populations, they sadly also show that, in spite of a very high average level of education of trans people, the past 4 years brought no noticeable improvement to the socio-economic status of members of trans communities.

3.3.5 *Transition & Self Expression*

The majority of male and female spectrum participants reported having started social transition. Of the respondents in the fluid spectrum, half were interested in a social transition. 4% of participants stated that they did not wish to socially transition; all of these were from the fluid spectrum.

Social Transition, by Gender-Spectrum

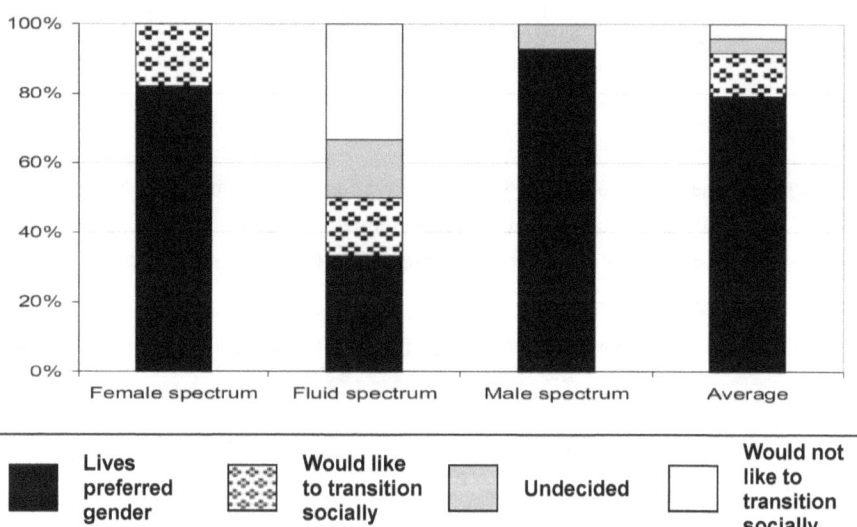

Meanwhile, 74% of participants had started to medically transition. 17% reported that they had completed all of their intended medical transition. 19% reported that they wished to medically transition, but had not accessed or had not been granted treatment. All but one of the respondents who reported that they still await to be approved for treatment were from the female spectrum. 9% of participants indicated that they do not seek to medically transition or had not made a decision; 75% of these were from the male spectrum[A].

Medical Transition, by Gender-Spectrum

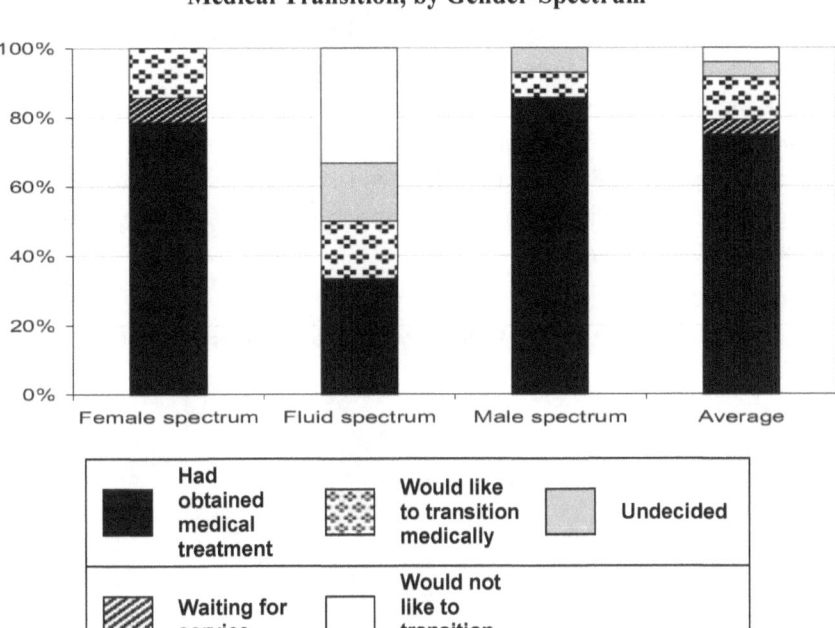

Most surveys do not report detailed data on social and medical transition, although many collect it. This makes a comparison to other surveys difficult and it is impossible to say if this data is in line or significantly differs from other research.

[A] *Based on the participants qualitative responses, it is unclear if some participants, especially from the male spectrum, interpreted 'medical treatment' as 'surgical treatment' and thus did not consider HRT as a medical treatment in their responses.*

3.3.6 Passing

Participants were asked to rate how often they felt they 'pass', and how often they experienced being acknowledged in their gender in two separate questions.

In the first question, participants were asked to rate how often they feel they 'socially pass'. Of the participants who lived their preferred gender full or part-time, individuals in the male spectrum reported feeling that they 'pass socially' far more frequently than the female spectrum counterparts did. Please note that the following tables do not report individuals from the fluid spectrum as it is not clear what 'passing' means to individuals in the fluid spectrum (see also 7.2.1), *'Transition' And 'Passing' In The Fluid Group.*

Self-Assessed Average Rate of Passing, by Gender-Affiliation

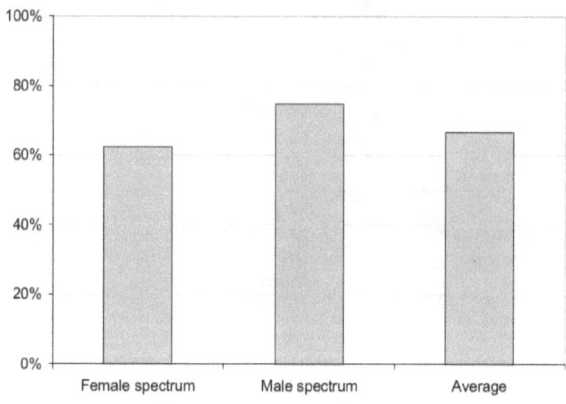

While the above chart lists the average reported passing rate, the next chart lists how many people reported a *specific* passing rate. As can be seen, self-assessed passing rates of 50% and 100% were lower in the female spectrum than in the male spectrum. Only a single participant (7%) in the male spectrum self-assessed that he passes less than 50%, meanwhile 31% in the female spectrum indicated a score of 50% or less.

Self-Assessed Rate of Passing, by Gender-Affiliation

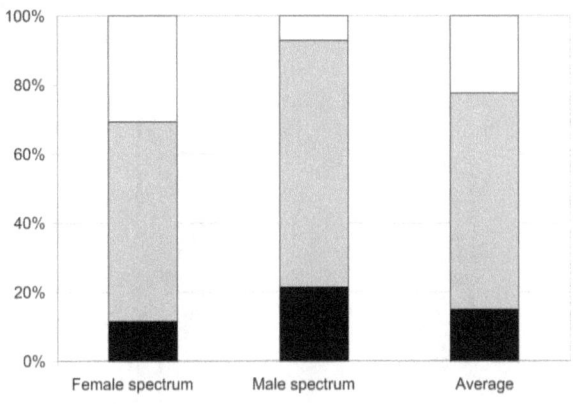

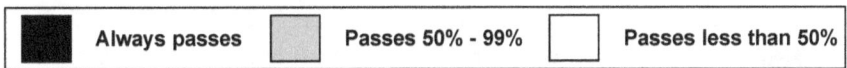

In a separate question, participants were asked to estimate how often they are accepted in their preferred gender. It is interesting to note that people feel more often accepted in their gender than they self-assess their passing rate (how often they *believe* that they are accepted as their preferred gender) for both female and male spectrum participants. This data suggests that individuals are more often accepted for who they are than they themselves believe. While the generally lower rates for female spectrum participants are repeated, it is noteworthy that the self-assessed and the observed passing rates are closer for female spectrum participants than they are for male spectrum participants. This can be interpreted as a more realistic self-assessment by female spectrum participants, or as an underestimation of how well most male spectrum participants in fact pass.

Self-Assessed and Self-Observed Rate of Passing, by Gender-Affiliation

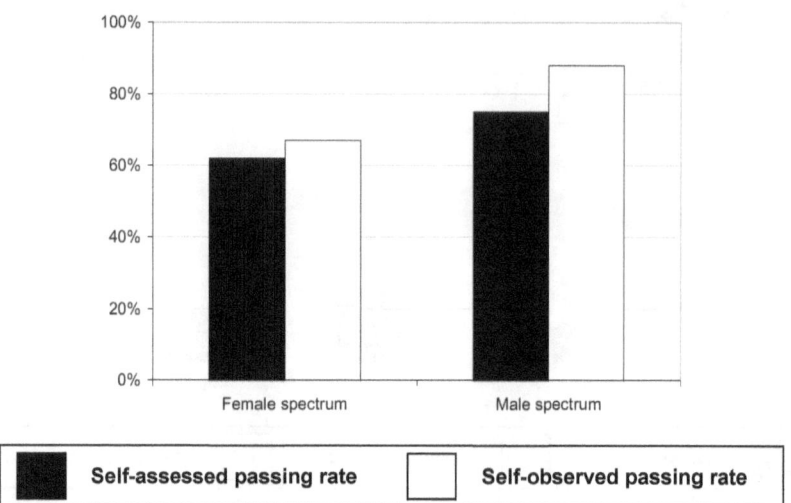

Again, it is difficult to compare this data with other surveys. Many researchers have stated that it appears to be easier for male spectrum participants to pass than it is for female spectrum participants, but few researchers support this claim with actual data. This survey corroborates the assumption that male spectrum participants indicate a higher 'passing rate' than female spectrum participants do, at least by self-assessment and observation. Once again this research appears to be well in line with anecdotal evidence from other research.

3.3.7 *Sexual Orientation*

Reported sexual orientations in this survey show a similar distribution to other surveys in trans populations (such as the TransPulse[76].or the NTCE[63,64] surveys), however the breakdown into gender spectra shows interesting patterns.

While Bisexual is a dominant sexual orientation in all spectra (in fact, it is by far the most reported sexual orientation in the female and male spectra), queer comes in as a clear second in the male spectrum, while pansexual is preferred in the female and fluid spectra.

In this survey an average of 7% of participants identified as asexual, while only 9% identified exclusively as heterosexual. This is unusual compared to other surveys, although in many reports (such as TransPulse[76]), it is unclear if the percentages reported indicate individuals who *exclusively* identified with one specific sexual orientation, or if they indicated a particular identification *as one of several*. Meanwhile, self-identified descriptions included "undefined", "complex", "fluid" and "other".

Sexual Orientation (Relative to Population), By Gender-Affiliation

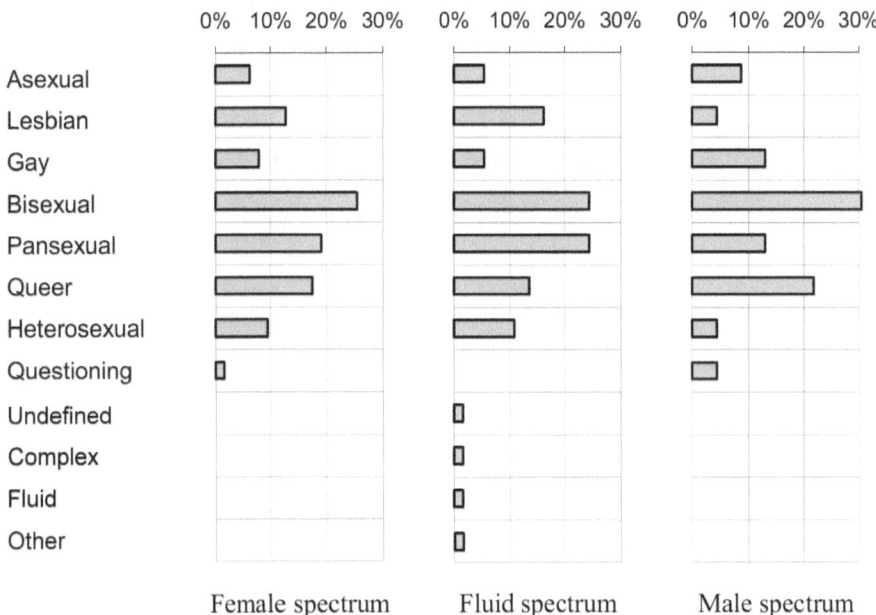

Female spectrum   Fluid spectrum   Male spectrum

Participants who used the Western sexual orientations of gay, lesbian, and hetero-sexual usually used these as their sole choice of self-description. Meanwhile, descriptions such as bisexual, pansexual, queer, complex or fluid were frequently used in combination. Due to the small sample size, this can at best be interpreted for a need of further research and not as a definitive finding.

3.3.8 Gender Self-Identification

Participants were invited to describe their gender self-identification. They could choose any combination of the predefined identifications in the chart below, or provide their own.

Many individuals in the fluid spectrum identified as genderqueer, but some provided their own identifications including "I do not identify along gender lines", "human" and "neutrios". Others provided self identified descriptions that are subtly different from the ones offered, such as "transfeminine" or "post-transsexual woman".

Gender Self-Identification (Relative to Population), By Gender-Affiliation

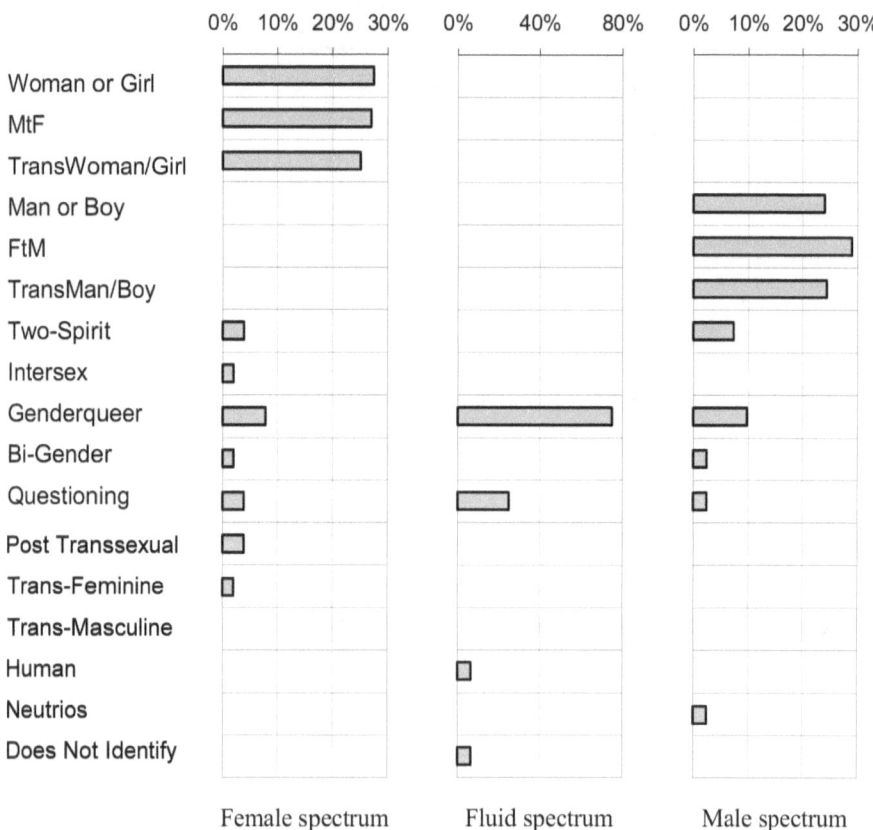

It is my opinion that many of the self-provided descriptions both from the sexual orientation as well as the gender self-identification responses from this survey should be added in subsequent research, in all useful gender combinations. While this may make comparisons to older research somewhat more difficult, I believe that reflecting the reported diversity and complexity of self-identifications in future research is an important form of acknowledging the feed-back provided by participants and a critical step away from current simplistic interpretations.

Once again, participants who used the binary identifications 'woman/girl' or 'man/boy' usually used these as their sole choice of self-description. Descriptions such as MtF, FtM, genderqueer, bi-gender, human and neutrios were frequently used in combination. The term 'post transsexual' was exclusively used in combination with binary gender designations. Once again, due to the small sample size this can be interpreted at best as a need of further research and not as a definitive finding.

Chapter 3: Comparing Data

Contents

► A short abstract on methodology and recruitment for the survey (3.1)

► How should data on gendered and non-gendered populations be reported (3.2)

► Presentation and analysis of basic demographic data (3.3)

Conclusions

► It is not meaningful to report data collected on trans populations according to an extension of birth-sex. Data on populations who do not accept such external gender designations instead need to be reported according to the self-identifications of participants.

► The data collected in this survey is comparable with other surveys on trans populations.

► The survey suggests that in the past 4 years, since the last Ontario survey, TransPulse (2009)[76], there was no noticeable improvement to the socio-economic position of trans people in the province.

4

THE BIG

PICTURE

4.1 The 3 Main Themes

Participants provided in-depth and rich replies to the main research question: how trans people themselves describe their own experience of being trans. In fact, due to the depth and richness of the answers provided, it is clear that additional participants would have contributed yet unseen topics and themes. However statisticians and social scientists would note that: the number of collected responses did not allow for a saturation of codes or themes[A].

Nevertheless, 3 main themes could be identified: 1. physical embodiment (including physical self-experience, body-image, physical self-acceptance, as well as medical treatment); 2. social acceptance and the lack thereof (including self-expression, external interpretation of self, social location, being defined by the outside and societal role satisfaction); and 3. self-finding (including self-understanding, self-acceptance, spirituality and self-realization).

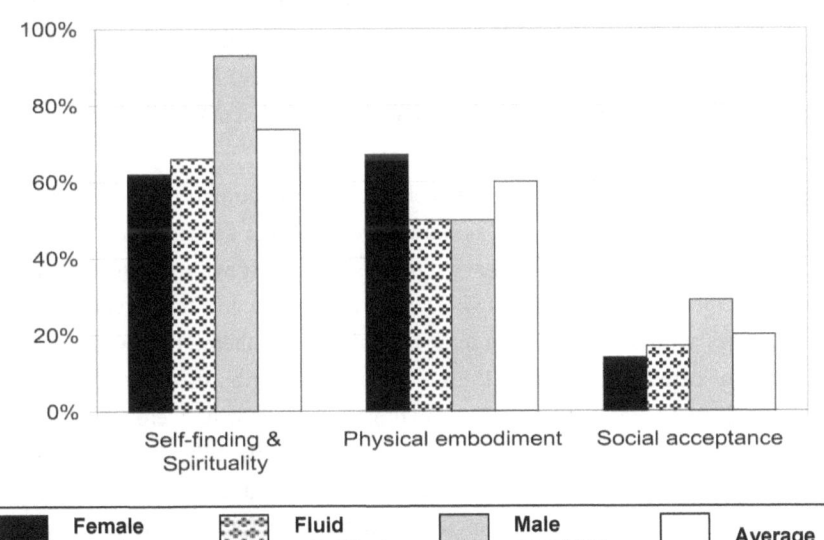

Frequency of Themes Addressed, by Gender-Affiliation

[A] *The term 'code' describes content of a specific nature in participant responses. The term 'theme' refers to a group of codes with similar meaning, or a range of codes that address the same topic. The term 'saturation' refers to a state where additional replies (from additional participants) are deemed unlikely to provide codes and themes that have not previously been identified.*

4.2 *Coming To Terms With Terms*

Before a more detailed exploration of these themes is possible, it is necessary to recognize that not all participants accept the terms 'trans', 'transsexual' or 'transition', or at the very least they do not feel that these truly apply to them.

For example, 35% of participants made direct reference to the term 'transition', or to before and after transition comparisons. The references usually related to SRS in the female spectrum, to HRT in the male spectrum. Relevant participant statements included: "post-op: that mismatched feeling is all but gone", "now I reside in my true woman's body and do not have to pretend anymore", "absolute contentment about who I am has replaced the constant anxiety I previously had", "my mind is now totally aligned with my female body", "I am a normal woman" and "changing genders has ended a lifetime of discomfort with myself and my relationship with the world".

Meanwhile, there was a small, but distinct group, 7% of participants, who did not relate to the term 'transition'. Participants stated that "I cannot say I have necessarily 'transitioned'" or "the feelings I feel are the same they have always been, nothing has ever changed". Some individuals in this group made it clear that 'transition' is something that is experienced (or constructed) *by outside interpreters,* rather than by themselves. An additional 4% directly stated that they do not wish to transition socially.

Some participants expressed similar feelings when it came to the use of the term 'trans'. While all participants had acknowledged that the term applies to them *in some way* by participating in the survey, or even explicitly with statements such as "being trans feels like being me", 15% stated that they do not, had never, or did no longer identify with or feel that the term is applicable to them. This was expressed as "[I] do not care for the 'label' trans", "I do not describe or think of myself as trans" and "[since SRS] I am not trans anymore". Respondents were very aware of the fact that the designation 'trans' is to some degree artificially created as a social construct: "I am 'trans' to the extent that I do not identify as the sex/gender that was assigned to me at/since birth" (female spectrum participant) - which of course means that the individual recognized that she had not been designated 'trans' (or been treated as such) if a female sex would have been assigned to her at birth.

4.3 One Community Or Many Communities?

While analyzing participant responses, it became clear that in the realm of self-experience (excluding social experiences), identifying one theme often prompted the location of another 'opposing theme'. For example, while some respondents reported a feeling of being denied any experience of sexuality before surgery, others reported enjoying sexuality before as well as after SRS and yet others stated that sexuality is of no importance to them. In another set of opposing themes, some participants described transsexuality as a self-identification, while others deemed the term merely descriptive of their situation and yet others stated that they reject being called 'trans' altogether or identified themselves as "post-transsexual". In a third example, participants reported that they either found solace in, didn't care for, or refused normative gender expectations.

Literally dozens of such divergent themes can be identified in the responses. This multitude can be interpreted as an indication of the fundamental diversity of experiences and of the diversity of trans people in general. It can also be interpreted as an expression of the complexity of individual experiences and of the subtle and detailed awareness of participants of this complexity. It furthermore shows why trans communities cannot be or become a single coherent social group. One cannot, for example, renounce gender as a concept and at the same time find solace in normative gender roles (see 7.1.1, *Societal Role Satisfaction*). One cannot define social transition as unwanted or nonexistent and at the same time as liberating.

Such fundamentally different interpretations inevitably socially distances individuals from each other. Various distinct groups form along the lines of mutual understanding, shared experiences, self-interpretations and self-expressions. In extreme cases what one group deems essential, another interprets as imposed and oppressive, or, in the realm of service provision, what is essential for one group is detrimental for another. Ultimately, members of groups who find themselves on opposing ends of many defining parameters of their respective interpretation of transsexuality may feel that they share little or nothing at all with each other, except for being called 'trans'.

The current clinical literature does not acknowledge or address this level of diversity or complexity. While some forms of gender-expression and diversity are well documented[8,9,10,21,22,23,24,25,71], the aforementioned, and many other aspects of diversity within trans communities receive little or no attention.

Some community authors are trying to disentangle the terms transsexual and transgender by suggesting that *transsexual* is not a subset of *transgender*[61], but to date even these limited attempts of deconstructing established ideas of hierarchies within trans communities have had limited success. Today, most authors at least implicitly assume hierarchical structures within trans communities. The interpretation that *no hierarchies or fixed structure at all* exist within trans communities, but that such structures are artificially created, is not discussed in the literature[57,58]. Examples include: neither *transgender* nor *transsexual* are a subsets of *gender queer*[A]; *transsexual* is not a subset of either *transgender* or *gender queer; lesbian* is not a subset of *woman*[B], not all *transwomen* are *designated male at birth* and not all *transmen* are *designated female at birth,* etc.[C]

[A] *Several participants stated that they identify transsexual, but did not consider themselves queer or gender queer or transgender, while others assumed multiple positions.*

[B] *Several participants who chose male as self-identification also indicated lesbian as their sexual orientation*

[C] *All but the last of these claims are directly supported by the survey. The last one is a logical extrapolation.*

4.4 Disrupting Systemic Beliefs

Fundamentally, the clinical interpretation of transsexuality rests on the premise that (a) clinicians have both the duty and the insight to correctly assign gender, and (b) that such assignments are always correct and thus must always prevail. The DSM's diagnosis of GID and the SOC's definition of 'transition'[79,80] are both based on the absoluteness of professionally designated birth-sex and gender. But as described in 2.3 (*Gender In The Service Of Heteronormativity*) and 2.3.2 (*The Euro-Western Pathological Approach*), both the designation of birth-sex as well as the subsequent diagnosis of gender, and with it that of a 'disorderly gender' (or of 'transsexuality'), are in fact based on entirely arbitrary criteria, completely excluding the self-identification as well as any emotional/hormonal or anatomical/sexual preferences of the individual. When enforced, such arbitrary definitions of gender create artificial limitations on self-experiences and self-expressions and in turn on self-identifications.

The artificialness of such limitations becomes very clear in the survey when a participant, who reported being designated female at birth, identified herself as *a male to female transsexual*. Such a self-identification is only possible when the birth sex designation is deemed subjective. In a clinical context an individual who is birth-designated female can only ever be a non transsexual woman or *a female-to-male* transsexual, but *never a male-to-female transsexual*[A].

If however this birth sex designation is subjective, and with it the 'from where' 'to where' designation in labelling transsexuality, then not only is the professional assigning of sex or gender at birth based on the looks of genitals absurd, but the SOC's requirements of 'transition' or the 'real life test' also are no longer sustainable. After all, if it is no longer known 'from where to where' a person 'transitions', then such a 'transition' can hardly be mandated or even be 'verified'. In fact, the entire definition of a 'disorderly gender identity' or of any related categorization in the DSM[2] as a 'disorder' can only ever be defined in relation to an 'expected order'. But if this 'order' is based on nothing else than arbitrary decisions and dictatorially enforced prejudice, then any derived 'disorder' becomes a scam.

[A] *Examples of individuals with a* female birth sex *who identify as* male to female *transsexuals include: 1) biologically intersex individuals 'female enough' to be medically female (usually determined by internal reproductive organs) but visually male enough to require surgical transition (e.g. have a penis), 2) female born individuals who identify emotionally and sexually male but prefer a socially female life (similar to a no-op male-to-female transsexual).*

However, if clinicians continue to insist upon the correctness of their approach, then *at the very least* the identification of this one participant will be severely curtailed. She will find herself excluded from treatment or be put into a position where she will have to lie for treatment. This could potentially put her in a position where she has to accept body-modifications (testosterone treatment and related f/m treatments, such as breast removal, as a 'permit condition' for SRS), or social interventions (such as forced transitioning to male, forced name changes or forced change of sex designations in legal documents) she may not otherwise have wanted.

While a single participant in a survey of 48 individuals may be an unreliable indicator to predict that 2% of the individuals throughout trans communities have similar identifications, it is nevertheless a reliable account *that such self-identifications exist.*

Individuals such as the one mentioned above exemplify and are proof that there is in fact no limit to the diversity of self-identifications and self-experiences or any combination thereof. This means that social, behavioural, legal or other external conditions for any related treatment, such as these described in the DSM[2] or the SOC[79,80], will by definition exclude and be directly oppressive and abusive to at least some individuals within trans communities.

Chapter 4: The Big Picture

Contents

▶ A first analysis of the qualitative question 'can you describe how being trans feels like' from the survey

▶ The section documents the enormous diversity within trans communities (4.3) and juxtaposes this diversity with the clinical interpretation (4.4)

Conclusions

▶ Participants expressed 3 main themes: physical embodiment, social acceptance (and the lack thereof), and self-finding.

▶ Many themes (or sub themes) addressed by participants prompted the location of 'opposing themes'. Such pairs of opposing themes were usually mutually exclusive. For example, while some participants felt that they relish in disappearing in gender-normativity, others felt that only by denying or subverting this normativity could they find and express themselves.

▶ The existence of such diversity and mutual exclusivity in many themes suggests that no one coherent trans community exists, but that instead trans is made-up of a great number of communities and individuals encompassing an amazing variety of at times vastly different self-interpretations, self-expressions and self-understandings.

5

SELF-FINDING AND

SPIRITUALITY

5.1 *The Most Common Theme*

The very fact that 76% of participants included statements that relate to self-finding or spirituality in a wider sense is noteworthy. Topics of self-finding, self-realization and spirituality formed by far the most commonly addressed theme, although individual expressions of the theme varied greatly. Interestingly, there was a clear preference of related sub-themes among the male spectrum with 93% of participants including the topic, compared to 66% in the fluid, and 62% in the female spectrum (see table on page 73).

It may be obvious that many participants address topics within this theme if one interprets living trans as a process of finding, interpreting and expressing a notion of self that is marginally acceptable by current social structures. Meanwhile, the SOC, the official clinical guideline of interpretation and treatment of 'transsexuality', offers not a single mention of the word 'spirituality'[79,80]. The SOC interprets the idea of self-finding and self-realization at best as a justification for professional intervention in the form of psychotherapy and then concludes that 'in severe cases' there may be a need for genital surgery as 'a treatment for a mental illness'.

The concept that the request for HRT or SRS could be *the result* of achieved self-finding, or an expression of the spiritual location of an individual is strictly denied. Any possibility of self-guided self-finding prior to requesting professional treatment is disregarded in that the SOC[79,80] mandates both psychiatric treatment, as well as waiting times on even the most emotionally and mentally balanced and mature individuals.

The self-finding on the level addressed by participants in the survey is of a profound, extremely personal and very individual nature. Participants spoke of deep self-finding, of life changing experiences, but also of pain, of breaking of relationships, of rejection, abuse and discrimination prompted by their self-finding and self-realization.

It is noteworthy that the theme of spirituality, self-finding and self-realization is the only one (excluding external social topics, e.g. social acceptance, see: 7 *Social Life And Transition*) that did not prompt a related 'negative theme'. Nobody stated that transsexuality would *not* be spiritual or include self-finding and self-realization. Consequently, topics of this theme become the most unifying of the surveyed group.

5.2 Self-Discovery

So what is there to be found in being trans? Participants spoke of "growing awareness", of "feeling more myself". They stated that "my experience will always make me different". They said that "I have grown from my experience and become much more open-minded and understanding than most people" and that "I have seen life like only a few [have] had the opportunity to see it", that "being trans is a deep knowing, not anything external" and that "this feels almost [like] a restoration, peace, a terrible wonderful work".

In spite of all the pain and hardship, participants clearly expressed a deep appreciation of their decisions to accept and express their feelings in saying that "I am very content living my true self" and that being trans is "something I would never go back on".

5.2.1 A Gift From Hell

A specific theme within spirituality was the extreme range of emotions people experience between pain and joy. Participants stated that "it's very painful being trans as I've faced so much overt discrimination", "I've been actively suicidal so many times because I was so hated by society in general", "it's often been very difficult and very challenging to even find the courage to stay alive" or "it's like being trapped in hell".

On the other side, there is "courage", "strength", "determination" and "self consciousness" that keep people on the path of seeking treatment in spite of all the adversity. Ultimately, after they have received treatment, their comments change to "after transitioning, being trans has felt like a gift", "after transitioning, being trans has felt very positive, increased my confidence and made me a more content person", or "changing genders has ended a lifetime of discomfort with myself and my relationship with the world".

5.2.2 A Place For Organized Religion?

Interestingly, none of the participants mentioned any type of organized religion. The theme of atheism was mentioned in a single contribution, but no other references can be found. Potentially, this is due to the small sample size, but it is also possible that current forms of organized religion have little to offer to trans people, individuals who are on a path of self-finding that is about as individual as it gets.

Another topic that is missing are conflicts religious beliefs often cause when individuals transition. Such conflicts could be prompted by gender transition or being trans in and of itself, or as a secondary element when such a transition leads to a re-interpretation of a previously heterosexual orientation to a homosexual one. Anecdotal evidence often suggests that conflicts exist within religious beliefs that are not accepting of homosexuality or transsexuality.

It is important to recognize that spirituality is not limited to beliefs that include God or Gods but includes many philosophical belief systems. Furthermore, just because an individual is not a member of a religious organization does not mean that they do not feel affiliated to it, just as the fact of being a registered member of a religious movement is not always an indication of actual practice or belief.

In our cultural evolution one could ask the question: how will organized religious institutions be able to acknowledge, accept and celebrate human complexity, and support trans individuals on their quest of self-finding?

5.3 *Self-Awareness*

Self-awareness describes a state of conscious experience of one's physical, emotional and, if desired, spiritual existence. It includes knowledge of one's intended self-realization, and a clear path to achieving this goal.

Several participants (14%) stated that being trans, or their physical or social transition respectively, are not a path to self-finding, but rather an expression of self-awareness achieved through past self-finding. The common interpretation of transsexuality the SOC offers, implies that a 'feeling of wrongness' leads transsexuals to seeking treatments. At this point, the SOC implies that only professional support can lead to self-finding. According to the SOC it is then the professional who is capable to determine if treatment should be granted to the individual, because only the professional can judge if treatment will allow the trans person a self-awareness that is experienced as meaningful. Meanwhile, the aforementioned participants insist that it is their achieved self-finding that leads to a self-awareness which, in turn, is interpreted as meaningless within their physical bodies and/or social roles. This then prompts them to seek professional attention solely because the treatment they know to need has to be sanctioned by a medical professional.

In this interpretation, the experience of being trans becomes both the reason for self-finding as well as the objective. Physical and social transition are no longer a goal in themselves, but rather become the means of expressing achieved self-finding. They do not create, but rather allow existing meaning to emerge. As such, members of this group report that both transsexuality as well as transition (at least if allowed to take place freely) are experienced as profoundly positive in that they create an environment in which it becomes possible to align the experienced self-awareness with the achieved self-finding.

It may come as no surprise that the above group reported having completed much more of their medical treatment than the average participant (89%). In other words, it is safe to conclude that the medical interventions of SRS and HRT allow the self-realization of some individuals by providing a self-awareness that is experienced as meaningful, and that these are also necessary to completing the self-realization. As the survey shows, individuals who had the opportunity to realize their self-finding and who have completed most or all of their desired medical or social transition stated "I relish being trans", living trans is "something I would never go back on", being transsexual "feels very positive", trans is "freedom", "I feel so liberated", or simply "freedom".

Unlike many others, participants in this group did not define themselves as 'survivors' or 'victims' of transsexuality. Instead, 85% of this group reported that they think of themselves as "no longer trans" or "never having been transsexual". In fact, all participants who defined themselves as not transsexual or post-transsexual were members of the above group. For these individuals spirituality and self-realization is a path of putting transsexuality behind, of finding closure and moving on. It also means that at least these individuals do not use the term 'trans' as a self-identification as they stated that the term does not, or does no longer, apply to them.

Of course, if one interprets transsexuality as spiritual, a path to self-finding and self-realization, then scientific medicine is ill equipped to determine what kind of self-realization matches any particular from of achieved self-finding, or what kind of self-awareness an individual should experience. After all, self-finding, self-awareness and spirituality are hardly medical conditions, the idea that they can be 'diagnosed' and 'dispensed as a treatment' is absurd. What individuals find on their quest cannot be 'predefined in a treatment standard'; doing so and mandating both the process as well as the outcome will only ever be experienced as destructive and abusive.

5.4 *Synergy And The Limits Of Language*

In the end, as has been acknowledged in the non-clinical literature many times, there is no common experience of being trans. Instead, the experience is highly individual and, according to some participants, by and large escapes capture, at least in the English language. Comments offered include: "I can't describe this", "[trans is] knowing who you are but not having the words to explain, they just don't exist" or

> "[being trans] is a holistic experience that cannot be reduced to any one dimension or factor. It isn't just about the body. Nor just about gender norms, expectations, and other social factors. It isn't just about spirituality, either. It's the sum of all the parts that come together to create a different kind of whole".

Ultimately, trans people themselves who have found healing through transition and treatment have difficulties accessing their own feelings prior to treatment, or to find adequate language to describe these. One participant puts it like this: "I find it difficult recalling the feelings I associated with 'transness' [before treatment]".

Chapter 5: Self-Finding And Spirituality

Contents

▶ Findings and discussion of the first major theme: self-finding and spirituality

Conclusions

▶ This theme finds contributions from 76% of participants.

▶ With 76% of participants including topics on self-finding, spirituality and self-realization, this main theme becomes the most addressed.

▶ Self-interpretations and the paths of self-finding participants mention vary greatly.

▶ The clinical interpretation and the conditions the SOC enforces upon treatment are experienced as greatly limiting and interfering with self-finding and self-expression.

▶ Some participants express the idea that being trans is the result of achieved self-finding. In this view, the need for medical treatment and transition become an expression of achieved self-finding, not the process through which self-finding is achieved. Members of this group often identify as *not trans*, *never having been trans*, or *post-transsexual*.

6

PHYSICAL

EMBODIMENT

6.1   Trapped In The Wrong Body - Or Not?

The well known saying that a trans person 'is trapped in the wrong body' could be located in the survey, but it was a clear minority contribution from fewer than 15% of participants. One participant used the description "[being trans] feels like being a woman born in a male body". Others phrased it as "before transition and surgery I always felt trapped" and "I just could not relate to the world with that body". Meanwhile, an equal number of participants offered contradictory interpretations such as "I don't feel like I am 'trapped in the wrong body'", "I think its my body, even when it felt alien", or very directly as "that 'not my body' stuff is fantasy".

Most contributions to this minority theme were, however, much more subtle descriptions such as "[my body] felt almost like a betrayal", "feeling an intense dissonance between your body", "[experiencing] a steady feeling of discomfort and general disappointment", "[experiencing] an incredible feeling of disconnect with my body ", "[feeling] disalignment and awkwardness", "I just could not relate to the world with that body", "I had never really acknowledged my body as being a part of me" or it felt "[like] an evil and sick sadistic twist".

There is no common experience of being trans, and no description of the experience every trans person would agree on. What initially may have felt like a brief description of a widely shared experience turns out to be a minority experience that is supported by some participants, contradicted by others and subtly adapted and re-interpreted by the majority. Ultimately, this theme appears to be more of a stereotype. If applied to the entire 'trans population' without context, as various authors and many media presentations on trans people have done, it will misinterpret many experiences, maybe even a majority. Nevertheless, it remains an important self-description of a sub-population, and thus can and should not be invalidated, even though it has been misused many times in the literature and in the media.

Ultimately, there is only one possible conclusion: such contradictory experiences are a result of human complexity, and in particular, of the experience of being trans. Once again, the experiences of people turn out to be far more complex than they are often presented.

6.2 *Our Bodies, Our Sex - It's More Complex*

With an overall contribution of 58%, more than half of participants provided a predominantly negative description of the experience of their bodies, at least before medical treatment. However, when looking at the data in more detail, the self-descriptions of participants once again turn out to be far more complex than anticipated. In this survey, participants distinguish between experiences of body-image, of disability and of sexuality.

Discussed Aspects of Physical Embodiment, by Gender-Affiliation

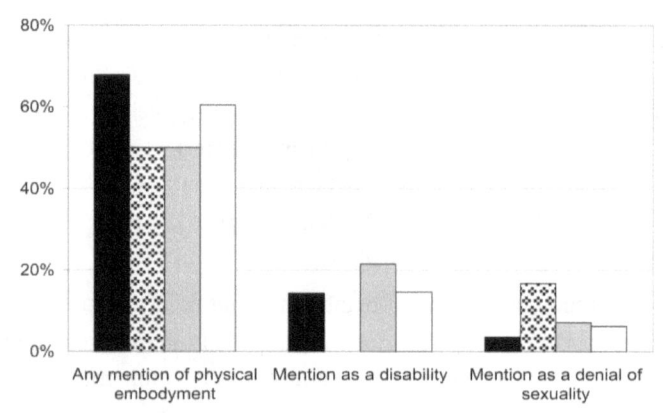

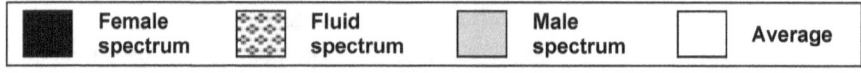

According to the responses, 15% of participants described the 'wrongness' of their bodies exclusively along the line of a physical disability, not as primarily a question of body-image. The very use of the word 'disability' to describe the experience of wrongness implies that this is about the body's *function,* not the body's *looks.* In fact, these participants noted that "being trans is like having an extra arm" or "its like not having legs and watching people walk around".

It is interesting to note that this interpretation was exclusively supported by participants from the female and the male spectrum (57% and 43% of contributions respectively), but not by participants from the fluid spectrum. It appears that participants from the fluid spectrum may not relate much to this interpretation of transsexuality.

Meanwhile, 7% of participants described negative feelings in relation to their bodies only and specifically in relation to being a sexual individual. One participant stated that "I cannot connect with the sexuality of my body and so I feel like I am denied sexuality". Contributions to this specific thread could be found in any gender spectrum, but were most prevalent in the fluid spectrum.

In many ways these two subgroups are reminiscent of the individuals described in 2.2 (*From History To Status Quo*) who, throughout history, did seek whatever interventions were possible at the time to correct either the physical or the emotional/hormonal experience of their bodies and their sexualities. Today, many individuals within these groups find their treatment needs denied through the SOC, unless they are willing to frame their experiences in a way that may not represent their true experiences, but will get them treatment. Furthermore, individuals may have to accept a social transition they would not otherwise have chosen and, in the case of an SRS-only request, individuals would also have to accept hormonal treatment and any and all experiences and related emotional and physical changes that come with this. If such conditions were imposed on prisoners for obtaining any form of medical treatment, surely this would immediately be called *cruel and unusual punishment*. But to impose the same on trans people can be done without hesitation. Few human rights organizations have yet to comment on it.

Some trans people resolve the dilemma of never qualifying for treatment through self-castration, others obtain 'illegal' surgeries (e.g. surgeries obtained on the 'black market', outside of the general medical system). But as this happens outside of the controlled medical establishment, no statistics on such treatments are available.

6.2.1 *'Self Policing' In Clinical Surveys*

It may not be surprising that participants who experience transsexuality in the context of a physical disability or a denial of sexuality reported that they are particularly unwilling to participate in clinical surveys. Overall 33% would not or would likely not participate. This increases to 75% in the female spectrum. This could be related to the fact that neither the clinical interpretation nor the SOC[79,80] accept such self-interpretations (see 2.2, *From History To Status Quo*) and that individuals feel left out, ignored or mistreated. Alternatively, participants may feel hopeless and disempowered in the face of the dominance of the current clinical interpretation and the power of the medical establishment. If so, their reluctance to offer contradictory self-interpretations in research would be detrimental in that individuals whose self-interpretation are some of the most contradictory to the clinical interpretation and the SOC would also be the ones who are least likely to make themselves available to challenge these assumptions.

This form of 'clinical governmentality', of 'self-policing of participants' by withdrawing from research, creates a self-fulfilling prophecy. Clinicians propose their interpretation. People who feel excluded by the proposed interpretation subsequently self-police by not participating in research, and potentially by presenting narratives that will give them treatment but have little to do with their lives. Clinicians then find themselves reaffirmed, finding only cases that represent their expectations. Consequently, for practitioners who solely rely on their clinical experiences, no need for inclusion or even challenging existing interpretations ever exists. Individuals who need a different treatment approach can be ignored as nonexistent forever, and the status quo need never be challenged (see 2.3.2, *The Euro-Western Pathological Approach*).

In any other field of statistical research, a *non-response bias*[A] of 75% (as this survey has found to be present in the female spectrum of this particular subpopulation) would immediately invalidate any assumptions held in regard to this population, and it would instantly prompt major questioning in regard to the soundness of the methodology and general assumptions underlying the research. In the past 50 years of clinical trans-treatment and trans-research, no such statistical review or even critical questioning has ever taken place. No research of this non-response bias has been carried out, nor any acknowledgment of this process in such documents as the SOC.

It is hard to believe that over these past 50 years of 'trans treatment' not a single research professional or author of the SOC would have been aware of this bias. It is even harder to believe that none of these professionals would ever have heard of any of the related self-identifications, or be confronted with these complexities. The fact that this is nevertheless completely ignored in the clinical literature as well as the treatment standards leaves one to question the scientific abilities of these researchers/clinicians.

[A] *"Non response bias" is a term statisticians and pollsters use to describe a bias introduced in research through intentional absence of groups of people who may hold a specific opinion.*

6.3 Beyond The 'Cross-Gender' Diagnosis

Another complexity within trans communities can be explored by investigating the clinical idea that transsexuals have a 'cross gender identification'[A], as is required for a diagnosis of GID. Clinicians apply the attribute of 'cross gender' equally to identifications, behaviours, expressions and experiences. But does this interpretation hold true?

As the chart (below) shows, 68% of participants mention gender in some form in relation to physical, social, medical, anatomical or other experiences or comments. Fewer participants (60%) directly mention some form of gender dissatisfaction, and even fewer point out that their dissatisfaction with gender is in fact a cross-gender preference (29%). Meanwhile, 17% of participants explicitly state that their gender dissatisfaction is not a cross-gender preference. Members of this last group often state that their dissatisfaction only exists in relation to their current gender (but with no specific target), or that the desired state is fluid, pan-gender, non-gender, bi-gender or other.

Reported Use of 'Gender', Relative to Population, by Gender-Affiliation

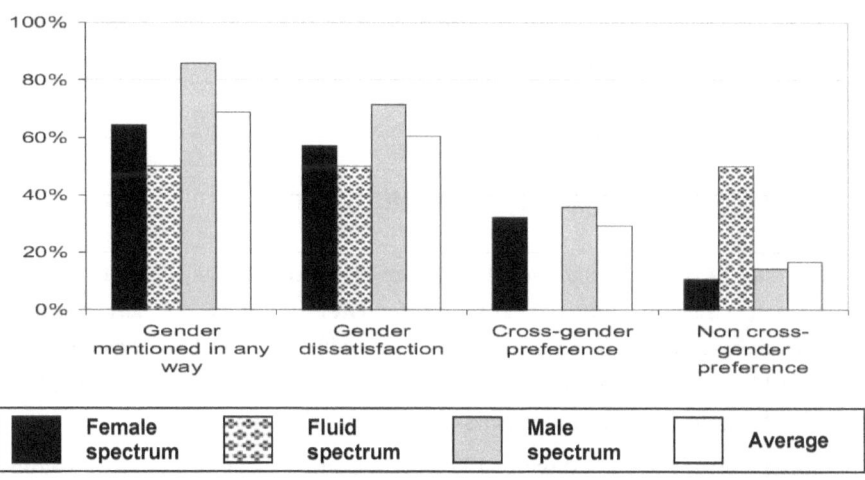

[A] *There is no definition in the DSM or the SOC of what 'gender', or 'cross gender' in fact mean, apart from the implied socially constructed ideology of the gender binary and medical assignment of 'sex' - none of which are scientific designations. Instead, the meaning of 'gender' and 'cross gender' is defined culturally, socially and individually. Consequently, these terms cannot be used in a standardized way. This is a fundamental limitation that should be recognized in both the SOC and clinical practice, and must also be acknowledged in this section of the study.*

Gendered spectrum participants mention gender significantly more often than fluid spectrum participants do. Female spectrum participants stated that "I am a woman in every way that matters", "an internal sense or feeling that female is my correct gender". Male spectrum participants stated that "[being trans feels like] being the wrong gender" and "my vision includes male sex characteristics". However, both the male and the female spectrum have significant populations with non cross-gender preference, relevant quotes include "it feels like I don't want to be like this", "[being trans is] feeling incongruent with the mainstream", "I like that I know there is an opt-out button [from gender], even though other people don't see it".

Meanwhile, none of the fluid spectrum participants mention a cross-gender preference. In fact their contribution is by far the most significant mention of a non cross-gender preferences (50% of participants from the fluid spectrum). Contributions include "I do not identify in terms of sex/gender", "[I am] non-gender identified" or "I adore that I can fuck with gender, confuse people, be both male and female at the same time, or neither". This is not entirely unexpected, after all, members of the fluid spectrum often do not accept normative gendering or reject the concept of gender altogether. Consequently, the concept of 'cross-gender' becomes meaningless to members of this group.

Sadly, individuals often professionally get labelled 'gender confused' if they do not live, or at least prefer, a clearly one-gendered identification, no matter if they position themselves in the fluid spectrum or if they prefer other forms of non-normative expressions. Within the medical gender-binary, the 'opt-out button' from gender as wished for by some participants does not exist.

6.3.1 Despite A Question Never Asked

According to the SOC, individuals who are provided with any form of medical treatment for transsexuality (prescriptions for HRT, referrals, and any restricted surgeries themselves) must have been diagnosed with *severe* GID[79,80] as described in the DSM. To be labelled with this pathology, the DSM itself requires individuals to exhibit "a strong and persistent cross-gender identification"[2].

In this survey, I have not directly asked participants to state if they feel "a strong and persistent cross-gender identification". However, as the SOC requires that individuals suffer from severe GID to obtain medical treatment and in turn any GID already requires a *strong and persistent* cross-gender identification, it could be expected that participants would volunteer such profound aspects of their personalities in any self-description, including the one of this survey.

According to survey responses, 75% of participants have started some form of medical transition. This means that at the very least these 75% of participants must have been diagnosed with GID and consequently must have been deemed to be 'severe cases of cross-gender identification' by treating physicians. However, in this survey only 17% of participants mention any form of distinct cross-gender dissatisfaction, identification or even preference. Meanwhile, a minimum of 58% of participants (75% minus 17%) have received a diagnosis of severe GID[A], but felt no need to include this 'severe, strong and persistent' feeling in their self-descriptions (see 2.3, *The Standards Of Care*).

This discrepancy is noteworthy. It further supports the assumption in the literature that a significant number of individuals 'align their narratives' to professional expectations in the medical office to obtain treatment (see 2.3.2, *The Euro-Western Pathological Approach;* 2.4, *The Privilege Of Being 'Properly' Gendered*). After all, to obtain a diagnosis of 'severe cross-gender identification', their narrative presented to the diagnosing physician must have been significantly different from the one they offered in this survey.

Various Usages of Gender and Genderedness

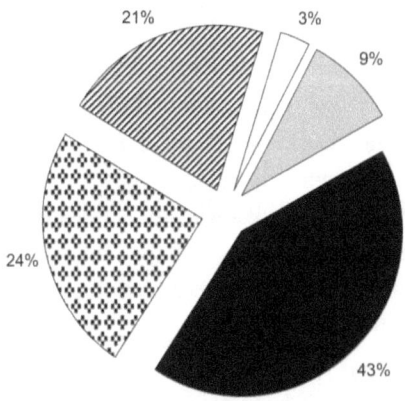

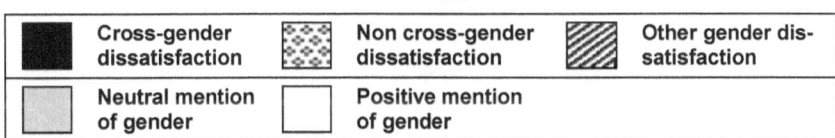

[A] *It is possible that additional participants have received this diagnosis, but not started medical treatment.*

The diversity found in the responses has significant implications. It is obvious that, while being expressed by the largest segment of this survey's population, cross gender identifications are by no means the only gendered identification mentioned by participants. As with the image of the transwoman as 'a woman in a man's body' (see 6.1, *Trapped In The Wrong Body - Or Not?*), the idea that all trans people suffer from 'a severe cross gender identification' is in fact somewhat of a stereotype to which trans people are expected to live up to. However, unlike the former, the latter is not just a social stereotype, but has significant clinical implications in that the DSM expects "a strong and persistent cross-gender identification"[2] as the very first diagnostic criteria. The SOC establishes that such a "strong and persistent cross-gender identification" must have existed for a minimum of one year[79,80] before any treatment (except psychotherapy) can be made available.

As mentioned before, 75% of participants reported that they have started medical transition. At the very least these participants must have been diagnosed with GID. Meanwhile, a total of 36% of participants directly state that they do not have a cross-gender identification. These consist of 24% of participants who indicated a distinct *non* cross-gender identification, and a further 3% and 9% respectively who reported either being pleased with their gender or having a neutral position. Clearly there is a diagnostic problem here for everybody who does not exhibit the required cross gender identification.

Severe discomfort with one's body or physical gender is a significant negative influence in the lives of many trans people, even if some participants may not have expressed such concerns in this survey. However, the presence of a 'severe cross-gender identification' may not be, as the DSM and the SOC imply, an all-encompassing, single minded criteria for all trans people. Other gender related, hormonal, philosophical or spiritual reasons may be of equal or even greater importance to some individuals. Until such time as treatment is available unconditionally, any assumptions related to this topic should be considered with caution, as both responses and interpretations may be tainted through conditioning by professional and treatment requirements.

It is important to note that not to accept one's assigned gender is only synonymous with 'having a cross-gender identification' in a strictly normative, binary gender system, such as the one the medical model promotes. As such, it is an assumption that is solely based on ideological limitations of the clinical interpretation and the medical model.

While the clinical interpreter may take this binary medical ideology for granted, this survey shows that, at least within trans communities, this model is not sustainable. Instead, it is oppressive, can lead to treatment denial and break-down, and has the potential to severely interfere with open communication in the medical office in that trans people may be scared to volunteer any personal information they know will contradict professional expectations.

Ultimately it is of little or no consequence who is doing the lying. It could be patients inventing a narrative for the benefit of the diagnosing professional (see related suspicion in the literature, 2.4, *The Privilege Of Being 'Properly' Gendered*). It could also be physicians lying on compassionate grounds by misdiagnosing trans people for the benefit of them receiving treatment. The result of a deliberate misdiagnosis still protects an abusive system that will require the next patient (or physician) to similarly lie. It furthermore prevents a real and truthful scientific re-evaluation as it propagates the belief that there is 'nothing wrong' with the established system, the underlying model, or the ideology it represents. Meanwhile, the true experiences of many trans people are erased by a system that appears incapable of dealing with the real-life experiences of many trans people.

Chapter 6: Physical Embodiment

Contents

▶ Findings and discussion of the second major theme: physical embodiment

Conclusions

▶ This theme finds contributions from 58% of participants.

▶ Stereotypes, such as 'trans people are born in the wrong body' are addressed. Participant opinions, once again, vary to a degree of mutual exclusivity.

▶ Being trans can be experienced as a disability. 15% of respondents express this interpretation, but it is only shared by female and male spectrum participants.

▶ Being trans can be experienced as a denial of sexuality. 7% of respondents express this interpretation and while it is shared among all spectra, participants of the fluid spectrum clearly identify more with this interpretation than any other.

▶ Many self-experiences and desired self-expressions contradict assumptions in the SOC. To obtain treatment, it can be expected that participants will have to adjust narratives and self-expressions to the conditions the medical system sets out.

▶ Respondents self-police participation in clinical studies. Members of the aforementioned groups, which do not corroborate clinical expectations, are far more likely to indicate that they would not participate in clinical research. In this survey, the non-response rate for female spectrum participants from the aforementioned groups is 75%.

▶ The clinical requirement of suffering from a 'strong and persistent cross gender identification' in order to be allowed treatment is contradicted by the reality of a great variety of self-interpretations reported by participants that are not 'cross gender'.

▶ The clinical idea of 'cross genderedness' is exposed as a cultural ideology maintained by normative professional beliefs, not facts.

7

SOCIAL LIFE AND

TRANSITION

7.1 *From Self-Definition To Social Prejudices*

Within the 2 preceding chapters, the main themes of self-finding and physical embodiment were addressed. These themes are intensely personal, and so are the difficulties and the solutions participants wrote about. The last main theme, social life and transition, extends the focus from the personal into the social. It also repositions the focus from the bio-medical into the political dimension.

It is clear that any form of self-finding and, maybe more intuitively, every form of medicine, is always political. This applies particularly to medicine in the use of enforcing social control and social standards. However, the social sphere introduces many other concepts that are less relevant on an internal path of self-finding and locating an emotional and physical state of harmony for oneself. These include: human rights, family and friends, legal issues, workplace adaptations, administrative hurdles and many others. This is no longer about how people identify themselves, it is about how people are identified by others. For trans people this means that if they do not fit into the socially expected gender presentation - which most trans people do not, at least for a time in their lives - then they are in danger of becoming subject to social prejudices, to ostracism, oppression, violence, or worse.

It is however interesting to note that, while both of the other main themes attracted contributions by large numbers of participants, 76% and 58% of respectively, only a minority of respondents addressed social acceptance. Overall, 20% contributed to the theme. This number rose to just under 30% in the male spectrum, but fell to only 14% in the female spectrum. It is particularly interesting that participants in the female spectrum, while reporting a lower self-assessed and self-observed passing rate (see tables on page 56 and 63), also comment a lot less frequently on their social life and social acceptance than male spectrum participants did.

Members of the gender fluid spectrum do not identify within the gender binary. In this survey, all members of this group stated that they experience a non cross-gender preference (see table *Reported Use of 'Gender', Relative to Population* on page 97). Any expression outside of the gender binary is likely to be interpreted as 'not passing'. Living within our society will therefore be a difficult experience at best.

7.1.1   *Societal Role Satisfaction*

Just as gender norms (or any form of normativity) can be experienced as oppressive or as reassuring and comforting, so can both the deliberate or inadvertent transgression of such social norms. About half of all contributors expressed relief for being accepted within their social gender once they fell within the preferred normative category and were recognized as such. They stated that "for me, it is very clear cut, as I identify both as a man in terms of my gender, and as male in terms of my sex" or "I'd like to just disappear into maleness". Meanwhile, others stated that "it's less about how I identify/feel and more about how I am read by others" or "you are living your life for others and not yourself" in acknowledging that the normative expectations felt both artificial and oppressive to them.

However, a significant group (33%) expressed discomfort or a disconnect with the concept of gender in general. Participants stated that males and females "are a blank space for me" or "I do not identify in terms of sex/gender". Some of these participants reported experiencing being trans as a liberation from gender norms: "I feel so liberated, so separate from gender norms and expectations, that I relish being trans" or "being non-gender identified, I can definitely feel how engrained (and ideologically driven, and oppressive) the two-gender/two-sex system is".

Once again, participants locate themselves within mutually exclusive ends of a theme. One cannot take solace in normative gender and at the same relish in subverting or destroying this strict duality. Again, participants show in their responses the complexity of the full spectrum of human experiences and expressions. They defy any simplistic categorization.

There was, however, a uniform notion by participants addressing the topic of societal role satisfaction that, even though many reported that they live relatively unhindered in their social role, none thought of themselves as completely socially accepted in every respect. Instead, participants reported either living stealth, or living with at least some difficulties in society.

7.2 Troubles With 'Transition'

Responses about the notion of transition reflect the complexities in trans communities. While some participants reported that *social transition* is very important to them, there is a significant subgroup that did not identify with the term or did not wish to transition socially. However, it is important to note that, while there is probably always a process where trans people become more themselves, one's own experience of this process can be very different from other people who observe it. What may not feel like a transition, or a deliberate process of change, can very well be experienced as such by an observer.

Nevertheless, some participants (6%) stated that it is *the social environment* that goes through a change of recognition and acceptance, of re-interpreting the trans person for who this individual has always been. Similar thoughts in regards to transition are also sometimes explored in self-help and some counselling literature[14,16,19,34].

The clinical approach meanwhile blames the individual for being transsexual and therefore expects the individual to re-adapt to the existing environment. Looking solely at the individual, the clinical process of transition can not be interpreted as a change of recognition by the environment, but must be performed by the trans person. Consequently, clinicians and the SOC strictly enforce and police a clearly visible, often stigmatizing and sometimes dangerous normative individual social transition[79,80]. In this interpretation, the choice of an individual to transition or not does not exist. Instead of the self-expression and self-finding some participants express as the motivation for transition (or for 'leaving' their assigned, stereotypical gender role), this clinical interpretation defines the wish to seek transition as the root cause of being trans, and then frames this 'wish' as a form of 'confusion' as it does not fit their interpretation of 'normalcy'. This alleged confusion then becomes the basis of the interpretation of transsexuality psychiatry puts forth, serves as the reason for clinical intervention, and is the grounds upon which the SOC and access to treatment are defined.

From the perspective of the transitioning individual, the notion of gender as an act[9,10] internalized through social training and behavioural conditioning has a lot of merit. Transition then becomes the process of unlearning gender conditioning and possibly of accepting a different form of conditioning. Although in trans populations the coercive nature of treatment requirements makes it unclear just how much of the observable behaviours are indeed a choice of the trans person, and how much is coerced by expectations of the treating professionals, or of the applied treatment standard, or of other related concerns that the individual may have. Ultimately the question is how much of the behaviours trans people exhibit are actual expressions or desired behaviours of individuals, and how much of these behaviours are performed to meet diagnostic expectations. In this scenario, the clinical dictate of social behaviours, such as 'transition' and 'the real life test' reduce 'being trans' to yet another form of coerced conditioning. This time it is a form of coerced clinical compliance instead of societal training.

Many trans and post-trans community authors[56,61,71,73] state that the clinical requirement that one must 'transition', the subsequent 'living as' and 'real life test' in order to access treatment (or at least SRS) as described in the SOC, are abusive. While the enforced process of transition[79,80] may be just what some people are looking for, the survey shows that, apart from aforementioned individuals, a number of participants from various sub-populations will have significant difficulties with this enforced system. Among these are participants who do not wish to socially transition or do not relate to the idea of transition (11%) and members of the fluid spectrum (13%) whose fluid, pan-, non- or bi-gender identities directly contradict the prescribed cross-gender identification of the DSM[2].

7.2.1 'Transition' And 'Passing' In The Fluid Group

As previously mentioned, the ideas of *transitioning* and *passing* have little meaning for many individuals in the fluid group (see table on page 97). In fact, asking questions along these lines can be interpreted as an act of reinforcing gender stereotypes on a group of people who have already made it very clear that they do not accept this categorization. In fact, this is one of the traps the simplistic 'one treatment approach fits all' solution SOC's[79,80] imposes. What may well be meaningful for some members of trans communities, in this case an enforced normative transition and a cross-gender identification, will be interpreted as harmful, indeed as a targeted exclusion for others.

This creates a research problem: how do we ask about something that on one hand the SOC demands, and on the other hand respondents in the fluid spectrum reported as meaningless, abusive, paternalizing and controlling? Asking these questions remains important in an effort to unmask and document the absurdity of enforcing a normative social transition on members of the fluid spectrum, as the SOC currently requires.

Important suggestions for further research are to: acknowledge this situation, make any related questions optional, and clearly state the reason for putting such questions forward.

7.3 *Living In The Wrong Society*

While many participants found ways to accommodate their needs within a gender normative society, others preferred to claim ownership of their situations in different ways. Instead of accepting the view of transsexuality as an individual 'illness', one participant stated that "I am trapped in the wrong society, one that has such narrow and fixed ideas about gender".

Others described their experience as "I like the term 'gender immigrant' because it encapsulates the ways we are only tenuously accepted in our new circumstances", "I think the term 'gender squatter' may be appropriate, because of all the backlash I constantly face".

One participant stated that "if you had parents from two different cultures, and were raised in one of the cultures, being transsexual is like a compulsion to live in the culture you're not fully experienced in but intensely knowledgeable of".

7.3.1 *Defined By The Outside - Or 'The System'*

Four participants (9%) expressed a feeling of *being defined by the outside.* They stated that the feeling of transsexuality is "[created by how gender is] understood by others and how you understand yourself gender-wise" or "I'm frustrated because someone else is making an unnecessary big deal about [being trans]". Others felt that "[transsexuality is created through society's] establishing and perpetuating essentialist ideas about 'each' gender". Transsexual is how they are seen or interpreted, but not who they are, or at the very least the importance of this interpretation or designation is blown way out of proportion in relation to what some participants felt it should be.

Clearly, participants do not feel universally accepted within society. Such acceptance, or the experience thereof, will vary greatly between individual participants. However, more than anything else, participants mention the unacceptability of a non-normative gender expression in a highly normative society. For some participants, such experiences may occur only for a short time in their lives, during transition, and then subside once individuals are passing and live stealth. Meanwhile, for others, in particular individuals from the fluid spectrum, such experiences of negative social attitudes - of rejection, ostracism, oppression and worse - will likely continue for a lifetime.

The individual experience of: the assault on one's core beliefs and existence, the fear and the loss of trust in social structures and institutions, and the experience of abuse, will remain for life. It does not matter how long such experiences persist, or if society will ever change as substantially as is needed to grow beyond enforcing or even expecting the strict gender binary. The experience of complete rejection for not conforming to social norms, of violent enforcement of such conformity, and of not being able to find a meaningful life in the box one is pressured into, will remain deeply embedded with the individual for life.

Chapter 7: Social Life And Transition

Contents

▶ Findings and discussion of the third major theme: Social life and transition

Conclusions

▶ This theme finds contributions from 20% of participants (30% in the male spectrum, but only 14% in the female spectrum).

▶ Self-experiences and actual or desired self-expressions vary greatly among the participants. Once again, several mutually exclusive themes can be located, re-iterating the previous conclusion that there can never be a single, coherent 'trans community'.

▶ Transition is not a term that is universally accepted. In particular for members of the fluid group, the concept makes little to no sense. This creates another rift with the clinical interpretation, and creates significant difficulties for accessing treatment.

▶ Prejudice, ostracism, oppression, threats and violence are routinely experienced by trans people, in particular by individuals who do not live stealth.

▶ Internalized oppression as well as the fears of recurrent abuse are themes within the lives of many participants.

8

A CALL

FOR CHANGE

8.1 More Than Science?

The survey shows several distinct groups within trans communities whose needs are currently invisible or not well documented and addressed by the enforced standards of care. Many authors, from clinicians[A] to a range of non clinicians and community authors[B], have put forward models of 'why trans people are trans'. Most of these models explain the motivations, self-identifications, self-expressions and the treatment needs of *some* members of trans communities, but not one explains all of them.

If, as the survey shows, even some transsexuality has a spiritual component, or if it is an expression of self-finding, then it will never be possible to compose a complete list of 'all valid trans identities'. There will never be 'a complete list of desired self-realizations', nor can there ever be a complete predefined scheme of support or medical interventions. After all, self-finding and spirituality have infinite possibilities.

Meanwhile, the scientific medical model is based on extrapolating the best treatment based on empirical data collected from past observations. At least this was the idea before the medical community decided that transsexuality should be treated without any such scientific rigor[C]. Maybe this happened in conjunction with the decision that policing social morality, such as heteronormativity and the gender-binary, ought to be a part of medical practice (see 2.3.2, *The Euro-Western Pathological Approach*). Even if trans treatment were defined solely based on scientific research and clinical trials, the problem remains that any treatment directed by science is fundamentally irreconcilable with unhindered, free self-expression.

Even if we would use the scientific method, it would not be powerful enough to explain what needs explaining. By definition of the scientific method, science collects data, builds a model and then interprets the model to predict future outcomes (or define treatment standards). As such, any *future* outcome predicted is always an extrapolation of *past* data. Therefore, science is never capable of building a model for *immediate, unhindered* and *free* self-realization. The definition of 'freedom of expression' (or of 'free will') fundamentally implies that such expres-

---

[A] *Benjamin[4], Blanchard[6], Lawrence[43], Money[54], Urban[77], Zucker[82]*

[B] *Stone[73], Bronstein[8], Feinberg[25]*

[C] *"To date, no controlled clinical trials of any [...] hormone regimen have been conducted". Quoted from the WPATH Standards of Care[80], page 41*

sions can at any time differ from what a scientific model would predict, the expressions would not be truly free otherwise. Science is a very practical and useful tool, but it may not be applicable to such expressions as free will or self-realization.

Ultimately, it is a philosophical position if one prefers to interpret 'living trans' as *an experience of the individual right of freedom of expression,* or if one prefers to interpret 'trans treatment' as *an expression of the professional right of medical practitioners to police moral standards.* Neither position can ever be proven to be correct using science. After all, such choices are moral imperatives, not science.

To address such moral imperatives, societies rely on social agreements about which choices should be made collectively, and which choices ought to be individual rights. In a Canadian context, these social agreements are The Canadian Constitution[12] and The Canadian Charter Of Rights And Freedoms[13]. These documents proclaim that the freedom of religion, of thought, belief, opinion and expression are guaranteed rights *of the individual.* This means that one's self-identification (which is a thought or belief), and the expression thereof, does not require proof and is not negotiable. The question that remains is how we, trans people, obtain these rights.

As discussed before (see 2.3.2, *The Euro-Western Pathological Approach*), the authors of the DSM and the SOC promote a very different interpretation, that of the right of medical professionals to exercise social moral control. Promoting their status as the sole gatekeepers for HRT and SRS may help medical professionals to remain in control of transsexual lives for years to come. But this results, as this survey shows, in denying at least some members of trans communities true self-realization, usually by oppressing those who identify, or would like to self-realize, outside of the professionally approved interpretation of who they must be.

Of course the treatments devised by professionals work for some people. They may even work for a majority in some way, although these assumptions need to be further explored in community based research. As only one medical system is legally, regulatory and medically sanctioned, and trans people are denied the right to seek care in other, more accepting medical systems, how can we change the legally sanctioned system to work for everybody?

8.2 *Implications For Professionals*

The survey carries several clear messages for professionals who work with trans communities. The first conclusion is that any description of a human experience, such as being trans, can never encompass the range and depth of people's experiences. Within social science, the knowledge that such experiences cannot be fully described is widely accepted and often addressed. But as the professional literature on transsexuality is at this time almost exclusively dominated by medical and psychological discourses, such considerations are dearly missing in the discussion and completely absent even in the newest edition of the SOC[80].

The diversity of trans populations clearly is a problem when it comes to a 'how to' beyond the usual 'trans etiquette' of accepting people's names, pronouns, people's preferred use of washrooms and other gender segregated facilities. These issues of equality and basic dignifying treatment are of great importance. Many also have a great symbolic value. However, having knowledge of basic human rights issues alone does not amount to understanding trans communities. In a community where the same experiences can be interpreted from oppressive to supportive by different individuals, no understanding of oppression will ever amount to a full understanding of the population. This is problematic in a system where competency is believed to be a concept that can be acquired through the study of theory, such as in cultural, ethnic or racial 'competency' - or in 'trans competency'. While these models of 'acquired competency' have been heavily criticized before[68,78,81], the survey makes it clear that within trans communities no such competency can even be defined as no coherent interpretation of 'a community' exists. This also means that there can never be 'advocacy for the entire community', but only advocacy *for parts* of trans communities. If we do advocate, then it is of the utmost importance that we do not advocate for one part of trans communities *at the expense of another.*

On a personal note I, being labelled 'trans' and having experienced transition and treatment, would not deem myself competent to understand, or even be able to relate to all trans individuals. Neither would I be accepted by everybody, not because of issues of race, ethnicity, education, status or belief - these only ever add more complexity - but *because of the inherent diversity of the experiences and the complexities among individuals themselves.*

8.3 A Hint To Medical Practitioners

What the survey shows above everything else is that trans individuals and their communities encompass enormous diversity and complexity. Self-experiences and self-expressions vary to degrees that these cannot be standardized, or even documented.

Medical practice operates on an approach to 'define a treatment standard' as a 'best practice' according to past findings. The same treatment standard will be applied whenever the condition 'has been diagnosed'. This model has been very successful in the treatment of many illnesses and injuries. However, it is my opinion that within 'trans' treatment the current process of diagnosis and standardized treatment is utterly destructive for many trans people. The problem lies less in the method, but rather in how it is used. The current SOC implies that there is 'one transsexuality', and then constructs 'a single hierarchy of needs'. All trans people who request medical treatment need to be sent on a path of psychological intervention, then HRT, then transition, then related surgeries, and finally SRS. The only option people have is to stop at any time and not seek the next intervention.

The mistake the authors of the SOC make is that they combine and link elements that should be independent. They create causalities and limitations that are not real, such as the idea that nobody could ever benefit from obtaining SRS before HRT, that everybody must transition in order to qualify for SRS.

Therefore, I call upon the medical community to abolish the use of the SOC, and to replace it with *separate* best practices and treatment standards (and, if professionals require this, independent diagnosis) *for each and every treatment offered.* In this way, individuals could qualify and obtain treatments in an individualized priority and order, without one being a precondition for the other. An individual could, for example, obtain SRS *and then* start to take HRT. Another individual could obtain a mastectomy (or male chest reconstruction) *and then* start to transition. Another individual could obtain SRS and *never* socially transition.

Such changes would be a very meaningful first step, both in accepting the diversity of trans communities and the individual needs of trans people. It would be a significant step in allowing trans people to realize their true identities and self-expressions. This is a recognition that there is not 'one medical condition', but that there are several independent expressions, one leading to hormonal treatment, another leading to SRS, another leading to transition, and so on. Individuals could independently require none, one or many.

8.3.1 Systemic Change

Ultimately, I ask for a revolution in the medical system. I ask medical practitioners to recognize that, when they treat the injured and the sick, it is reasonable to base treatments on the scientific model of diagnosis and treatment. After all, illness and injuries can be scientifically defined and biologically, biomechanically or biochemically diagnosed. As such, the assumption that an illness or injury can very likely be treated best with an intervention that has worked well for the same condition in the past is reasonable.

However, I also ask that medical practitioners recognize that there is another field of medicine. In this field, medical practitioners provide access to wellness. But unlike sickness, which can be scientifically diagnosed and treated for 'humans' as a population, wellness is individual. It is emotional and cannot be understood through or defined by science. Wellness is not a state (such as biological health), it is a constantly changing process of being able to live life to its full potential. As such, the experience of wellness is individual to each and every person. Just as wellness is individual, so are the needs to achieving it. Sometimes, achieving wellness includes medical interventions. But these medical interventions cannot be diagnosed and then provided through a standardized process, they can only be individually identified and provided on an equally individual basis.

Finally, I ask that medical practitioners recognize that 'trans treatment' does not treat an illness. Trans people who ask for medical treatment do so because they need this treatment to live their lives to its full potential. Medical practitioners can provide the requested treatment as a prerequisite for the trans person to achieve wellness. But wellness cannot be defined by medical practitioners, or by a protocol, or a treatment standard. It is individual. In trans care, treatment choices must be left to trans people themselves.

8.4 Honouring People's Self-Realization

So what can professional service providers do? Being trans, according to the self-descriptions of 76% of survey participants, is about self-finding and self-realization (see chapters 4, *The Big Picture;* 5, *Self-Finding and Spirituality*). Therefore treating professionals should support individuals in their self-finding in a way that trans people can become who they truly are and realize their full potential.

Yet, as we have seen, things are not that simple. While all trans people have the general right to free self-realization, expression and belief guaranteed by the Canadian Constitution[12] and the Canadian Charter of Rights and Freedoms[13], they practically find these rights denied, and their lives heavily policed and interfered with. They live in a society that is often not accepting or even overtly hostile. They have to deal with social structures that don't allow for many of their most basic needs. Professional service providers are part of these structures. All professions in social fields have been and still are, to varying degrees, heavily implicated in processes of policing individuals and of denying rights to individuals in an effort to promote social control[26,38,51,70].

For many people in trans communities, transition and any related treatment could be one of the most joyful and life affirming experiences. If only our lives could be lived freely, according to our own identities, respecting our individual beliefs, needs and ways of self-expression. We can see this in the survey when participants state that being trans has felt "like a gift", "very positive" and that it is, or leads to "freedom". But as long as helping professionals control the lives of transsexuals, provide 'mandated help' for the sake of putting a checkmark on paper because some protocol 'requires' it; as long as professionals police and enforce lifestyles and dress-codes and call this 'treatment' and 'helping people'; as long as they decree that made-up rules, attitudes, beliefs and professional requests or requirements are more important than people's lived experiences and their actual self-realization; we will instead get many responses such as "transitioning is a very disruptive process" or "I will never erase my psychological trauma" or "I still [feel] depressed, but now more from having to deal with all the baggage accumulated from transition".

Many professionals are uniquely positioned to support people from trans communities in their self-realization. Professionals can be allies, supporters, activists. They can stand-up for social justice, for more research, for social change, for scientific instead of moralistic approaches, for transformation of their respective systems and ideologies. So no trans individuals will ever have to say again that they are "not living life to its full potential" or "[I am] being denied my true identity".

For this to become possible, any support needs to be given without an agenda of social control. Any social control imposed by supporters will deny the individual truly free self-finding and self-realization. When having their self-identification, their transition and their treatment policed, controlled, directed or even 'examined', then all that some trans people can achieve is to transition from one imposed identity that is not their own to another identity that does not truly reflect who they are either. For some individuals this may just work. But for people who experience the core of being trans as finding themselves and living what they find, any control of self-realization will defy the very purpose these individuals assign to their lives.

Chapter 8: A Call For Change

Contents

▶ What if the experience of being trans escapes a scientific interpretation (8.1)?

▶ Redefining trans treatment from 'curing an illness' to enabling wellness (8.3)

▶ Recommendations for professionals

Conclusion

▶ Trans treatment cannot be explained within the scientific medical model of diagnosis and treatment because the request for treatment, and living trans are expressions of free will, not expressions of illnesses.

▶ Trans treatment is the provision of wellness, not the treatment of an illness.

▶ The free, unhindered self-realization of the trans person must be at the core of support, treatment, policy and advocady.

▶ Living trans, becoming oneself and obtaining treatment (for those who seek it) could be one of the most positive and life affirming experiences if social attitudes and professional interpretations would allow it. To make this possible, we need social change, a professional reorientation and a new interpretation of ourselves.

9

EPILOGUE

9.1 Since The Survey Closed

As I have mentioned before (see page IX, *A Personal Retrospective*), I have received many e-mails in relation to this research. Since the survey closed, I have continued to receive contributions from members of trans communities which, sadly, I could not use due to the limitations of the consent condition in the ethics approval. However, the contributions I have received all reaffirm the following:

▶ The data collected in the survey is just a start. There is far more diversity in trans communities yet to be found and documented.

▶ It has become apparent that for some individuals their trans experience intersects with interests and identifications in communities outside of the trans spectrum. These include martial arts, fetishism, BDSM, polyamory, paganism and many others. How such intersections may change the experience of being trans and how this in return influences trans communities needs further research.

▶ Some people clearly appear frustrated with research in which they have previously participated in. Consequently, in several e-mails, individuals have expressed the hope that my research will be transparent and that I will in fact make results of my research available to trans communities within a reasonable time.

▶ Several individuals have complained about the short participation time of only 2 weeks. This was unavoidable within the confines set for a Master's level Practice based Research Paper, both in terms of not having the time to extend data collection, as well as of being limited in regard to the number of responses I was able to analyze.

▶ In a similar theme, several e-mailers made note that they would have liked to participate but that they lived outside of the catchment area, which was limited to the province of Ontario. Individual comments arrived from several Canadian provinces, a number of US states, and from as far away as Germany and Australia.

▶ Many contributions noted very positively that this research was carried out by a member of their own communities. Some felt reassured by the fact that I, as the researcher, am neither financially nor professionally linked to service providers to trans communities.

It is clear that many members of our communities are interested in research, that they are eager to participate, and that they more than anything else, are interested in truly independent, community based research.

9.2 We Should Know Better

It has been over a century that trans issues and trans lives have been studied by members of the medical community[35]. During this time, humanity has evolved from a horse and buggy culture where the telephone and electricity were novelties to one where space flight is routine, the internet is available worldwide and science is exploring the limits of the universe, both large and small. Meanwhile, when it comes to understanding transsexuality, not much has been achieved. Indeed, at times it feels that with all the dogmatism and the doctrinary ideologies from the 50's to the 90's and beyond, there seems to be less understanding now than what can be found in the books Magnus Hirschfeld published a century ago[35].

This is indeed sad. It is also telling. Trans people are not a priority. Studying trans communities and issues is not seen as the glorious high-end science that makes headlines (and gets top research dollars, or any), even though millions of people worldwide could benefit from a better understanding of trans lives. One could argue that this has much to do with the still prevailing transphobia, homophobia and misogyny, or maybe with a more general phobia of 'sexual alternatives'. Positioning transsexual individuals on the fringe of the socially and sexually allowable is an interesting notion. After all, for many transsexual individuals, 'integration into normative society' (e.g. 'passing') is the ultimate goal and, according to this survey, most trans people do not experience transsexuality as a sexual issue (e.g. one defined by sexual attraction or sexual activities).

The little actual research that has been done by individuals from outside of trans communities (often people with a counselling, medical or psychological background) lacks clear insight. For example, data on trans people is still routinely reported according to birth-sex, instead of according to self-identified gender (see 3.2, *Reporting On Gender Affiliations*). Both questions and interpretations are often limited by interpretative frameworks, professional ideologies or lack of imagination.

Trans communities can't rely on external research. We have done this for the past century. The result is a distorted interpretation leaving out many populations within the trans umbrella, and a 'one fits all' treatment approach for individuals who need medical treatment. This is not acceptable. We need a better understanding of trans lives, a better documentation of the diversity and the complexities in our communities, and a better approach to treatment. We need support and solutions based on the needs of individuals, not the ones based on dogma and professional ideology we have at this time. To break free from such dogmatism, to go beyond the status quo, to leave professional ideological limitations behind, to see past normative interpretations, community based research with no link to such dogmatic thinking and ideologically formed interpretations is necessary.

Sadly, to date no university or social service provider to trans communities has shown any interest to expand on this research of diversity and complexity in trans communities. My own requests to do this as a university based research project in the form of a Ph.D. has been declined by several institutions. Although universities do not give direct feedback on declined applications, it can be guessed that they would deem the results of such research as potentially very inconvenient for both theorists and clinicians. After all, if research would find that to reach their full potential, and have a high quality of life, trans people need highly individualized support and treatment, then all of the current one-explains-it-all theories, and the single minded one-fits-all approach to clinical treatment would be in jeopardy. This is particularly true if the research would also show that there is no universally shared motivation of trans people, but that many motivations for any and all of the expressions within trans communities exist. As such, the rejection of such research on a larger scale is probably a sign of how obvious it is that this diversity and complexity exists, how significant the subsequent changes to both theory and clinical practice are estimated to be, and, most importantly, how inconvenient acknowledging this diversity and accommodating such knowledge could turn out to be.

If professionals can't be trusted to perform science in a reasonably objective and neutral manner, if they can't be trusted to accept results even if these contradict their ideologies, or if they can't be trusted to use the scientific method at all, then we, the members of our trans communities, are once again left in the position to educate the professionals. Not that this is a new experience for many trans people...

9.3 Some Final Thoughts

Trans lives are complex. There are no instant solutions and no quick fixes to most problems trans people encounter in their lives. But as my research has shown, there can never be a 'one fits all' strategy that will be supported by all members of trans communities.

Instead of presenting 'omnibus solutions', initiatives should be kept small, they should be discussed, or even better, directly originate from trans communities. But most importantly, all initiatives, options, laws, or services offered should be *on an opt-in basis* so individuals are free to accept or reject these. At the very least, any and all services or programs offered must be offered independently, opting out of one avenue of support, treatment or pseudo-requirement *can never have an impact for the consideration for another.* For example, a person's specific lifestyle cannot be a consideration when it comes to providing any form of medical treatment.

Only when systems are taken apart, by offering services individually to trans people, can coercive behaviours be dealt with. However, coercion is not the only issue that needs addressing. Combining several services in personal union can create a conflict of interest, either for the professional or the trans person. For example, a trans person can perceive a conflict of interest if the same individual provides both prescriptions for HRT and some other form of health care. This can lead to a situation where the trans person no longer feels free to volunteer health related information, fearing that this may compromise access to HRT. For example, a trans person may suspect they are suffering from a form of cancer (e.g. breast cancer), but not disclose this in fear that the physician will cancel HRT as estrogens are known to sometimes promote the growth of such cancers. This effectively sabotages the provision of meaningful and effective healthcare.

More fundamentally, who we are and what gender we live and express are human rights, not decisions medical practitioners can, or should make. Human rights exist inalienably, and can not come at the discretion of a physician. Exercising a human right may not be healthy. However, we still have the right to exercise these *at our own discretion.* Exercising the right to free speech or the right of free assembly can, depending upon the circumstances, be very dangerous, even deadly. Nevertheless, exercising these rights and accepting such dangers must be our own decision, not the ones of the police, a judge, or a healthcare provider. As long as transsexual individuals have to ask for a permit from a physician to be allowed our self-experience and our self-expression, we do not have the same basic rights other people have. Instead, we are controlled, policed, and limited. While everybody else's rights are inalienable, ours remain revocable at the stroke of a pen. While everybody else's lives are unconditional, ours are re-evaluated every few month by an individual who claims authority over our self-identifications and then decides if we deserve these for another few months or not.

First, we were assigned a gender that was not our own by medical practitioners who deemed themselves omni-competent to assign gender to everyone at their sole discretion. This did not work for us. When we stood up and demanded out rights to self-realization, another part of the medical system assumed competency over our lives, demonizing us and controlling us by declaring us mentally ill. After we protested this too, yet another branch of the medical establishment rose up, insisting that there is a need to judge, limit and regulate our identities through a 'professional standard', and to control the means of our self-realization for life. For many, this looks like nothing else than a continued change of abuser, with the same abusive intention: to find yet another ruse to reject our identities, to construct another justification to control and limit our self-interpretations and our self-expressions. To limit our diversity and the complexity of our self-interpretations. This is not a fundamental change, and it certainly is not progress. It is simply another disguise for the same old abusive dictate that we cannot truly be who we are. After 100 years of trying, is it finally time to realize that the healthcare system is not capable to provide meaningful trans related services to us because of the very methods and thinking that make them so successful elsewhere?

Such experiences impact individual trans people very differently. This is why support, medical services and the provision of long-term treatment must be tailored to the individual needs and interpretations of each trans person. But once again, the key is that it is the individual, not a professional, who must be given the rights and the options to choose according to their needs. Ultimately, this is the only way to respect, accommodate, value and foster the enormous diversity within trans communities. Trying to define yet another 'system that will work for each and every individual' is futile and will, just as previous iterations of the same ideology, prove to be highly destructive, at least to some members of the communities.

Finally, the systems society puts into place must be adapted to the needs of the people they serve. As long as we continue to instead adapt people to systems, if need be by service denial, coercion, or even force and violence, we will fail people for the sake of maintaining outdated systems and outdated thinking.

We need systems to serve people, not people to serve systems.

Chapter 9: Epilogue

Contents

▶ Experiences during the research

Conclusion

▶ There is continued interest for this research in trans communities.

▶ There is a great lack of trans research.

▶ Many individuals have lost faith in clinical research or in the interest clinicians, governments and the healthcare industry has in them.

▶ Many members of trans communities are very interested in community based research. People are eager to participate and are looking forward to independent and not ideologically filtered results.

A

APPENDIX

A.1 Reading Charts

Most charts in this report are pie charts or bar charts. The first type of charts used, pie charts, report a distribution where the entire pie represents 100%. The percentages for individual segments are indicated near the segments and always add up to the full 100%. A legend describes the individual segments.

Pie charts are used where a single set of data (such as 'Reported Gender Affiliation', see example below) is presented, and all segments can be identified (e.g., there is no 'other' segment)

Reported Gender Affiliation (chart from page 53)

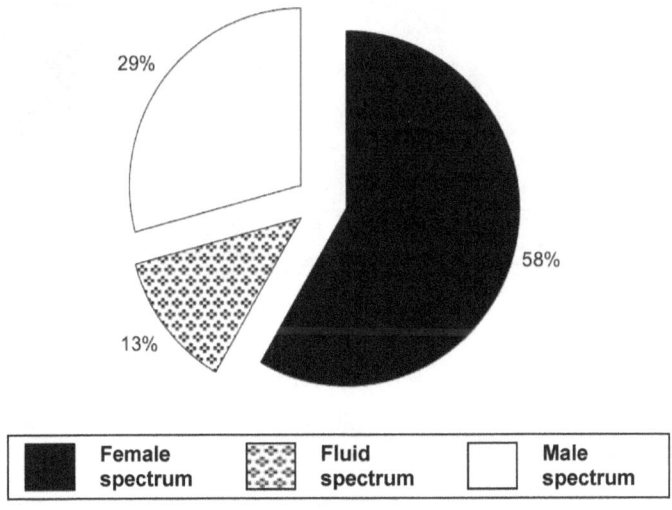

The second type of charts in this report are bar charts. Bar charts are used to present sets of data where it is not meaningful or possible to report 'other' (for example, where 'counts of participants' are reported), or when more than one set of data needs to be compared side by side.

Bar charts display data, whenever meaningful, by gender affiliation. The gender affiliation can either be found in the legend, or as a separation of bars in the chart itself.

The y-axis (vertical) of bar-charts can be a range of values (in horizontal bar charts, example see page 65), but more typically it indicates a percentage. Unless otherwise indicated, the percentages displayed are calculated *relative to the gender spectrum to which participants affiliate.* In the chart below this means that about 17% of participants *of these affiliated with the female spectrum* reported to be 18-30 years old.

Age Distribution, by Gender-Affiliation[A] (chart from page 56)

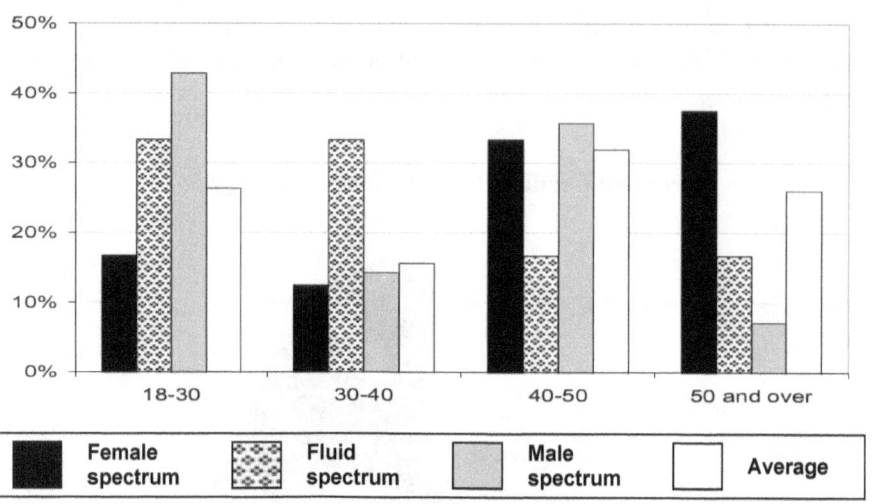

Whenever meaningful, averages are provided. Averages are weighed by the number of participant in each gender spectrum, giving each gender spectrum an equal total weight in the calculation.

Bars are grouped to facilitate comparisons, in the example by age group, to highlight the difference in age reported by participants from the gender spectra. The above shows that participants in the fluid and the male spectrum tended to be younger than participants in the female spectrum.

[A] *Please note: all averages are weighed by the number of participants in each spectrum.*

A.2 The Yin/Yang Fractal (Cover)

In Chinese philosophy Yin and Yang are generic symbols of opposites in nature. The Taijitu (the traditional symbol for Yin and Yang, also known as "Yin/Yang") symbolizes a unity of these opposites by combining both: two halves, a combination of contradictory aspects which nevertheless are similar in many ways and are both necessary parts to form a complete Circle of Life.

Taijitu (from Taoist and Neo-Confucian philosophy)

The black part (Yin) represents passivity, darkness or night, it is consuming and symbolizes femininity. The white part (Yang) stands for activity, brightness or light, it is producing and symbolizes masculinity. There are many other interpretations, traditional opposites such as fire vs. water, air vs. earth or sun vs. moon, just to name a few.

Each of the two parts of the Taijitu is a perfect half of the whole called 'unity'. While each half is an ideal of an absolute, they are both exactly equal in area and shape. Each also contains an element of the other (called 'seed'). While each half symbolizes *an absolute extreme* that absoluteness never truly exists in nature because every expression of any extreme *always contains a part of its opposite* and cannot exist without it. In nature Yin and Yang are in constant movement, change and interaction.

The Fractal version of the Taijitu introduces infinite diversity and complexity, while maintaining the idea of two identical halves, each containing a seed of the opposite. But the sharp division between the two halves disappears; each half now extends into the other. Indeed, the exact location of the separation is no longer discernable (the closer one looks, the more details appear). Both the edge of the seeds as well as of the unity itself are no longer sharp, but they maintain their distinctness. As a recursive fractal, the delimiting border of the seeds are now re-interpretations of the border of unity. The two seeds recursively become unity, each of them becoming a complete Taijitu with equal complexity, but differently shaped than their defining unity.

Yin-Yang Fractal

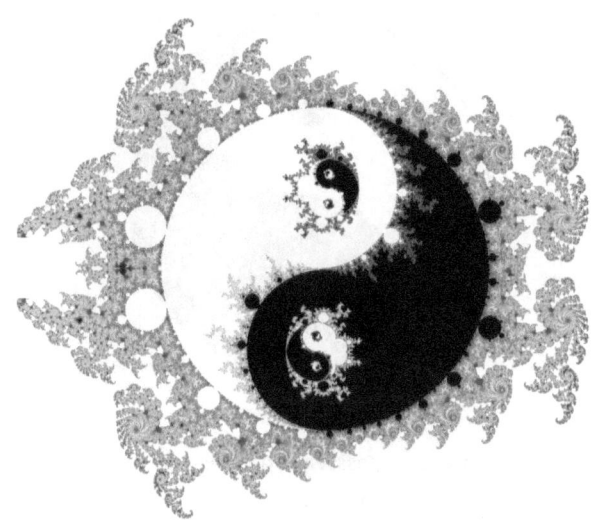

From a distance, the fractal border between Yin and Yang still establishes a clear separation. On closer examination however, this border becomes infinitely diverse and exceptionally complex. While a separation can be guessed, it can never be exactly positioned, nor measured. By increasing fine details, the complexity also increases. But the complexity always remains greater than what is currently visible, just as in the understanding of gender presented in this book (see 2.5, Social Theories - Not Quite There Yet). Meanwhile, the philosophical ideals of equality, symmetry and congruence of Yin and Yang are maintained, even in the infinite complexity the fractal creates.

A.3 The DSM's Gender Identity Disorder, GID

In the DSM IV-TR[2] Gender Identity Disorder [GID] is listed as Condition 302.6, for children, and 302.85, for adolescents and adults, it comes under the heading 'Sexual and Gender Identity Disorders'.

The DSM describes GID as follows: "Individuals with this mental disorder are uncomfortable with their apparent or assigned gender and demonstrate persistent identification with the opposite sex"[2].

The DSM IV-TR diagnostic criteria of GID are as follows:

A. A strong and persistent cross-gender identification (not merely a desire for any perceived cultural advantages of being the other sex). In children, the disturbance is manifested by four (or more) of the following:

(1) repeatedly stated desire to be, or insistence that he or she is, the other sex.

(2) in boys, preference for cross-dressing or simulating female attire; in girls, insistence on wearing only stereotypical masculine clothing.

(3) strong and persistent preferences for cross-sex roles in make-believe play or persistent fantasies of being the other sex.

(4) intense desire to participate in the stereotypical games and pastimes of the other sex.

(5) strong preference for playmates of the other sex. In adolescents and adults, the disturbance is manifested by symptoms such as a stated desire to be the other sex, frequent passing as the other sex, desire to live or be treated as the other sex, or the conviction that he or she has the typical feelings and reactions of the other sex..

B. Persistent discomfort with his or her sex or sense of inappropriateness
in the gender role of that sex. In children, the disturbance is manifested by any of the following: in boys, assertion that his penis or tes-
tes are disgusting or will disappear or assertion that it would be better
not to have a penis, or aversion toward rough-and-tumble play and rejection of male stereotypical toys, games, and activities; in girls, rejection of urinating in a sitting position, assertion that she has or will
grow a penis, or assertion that she does not want to grow breasts or
menstruate, or marked aversion toward normative feminine clothing.
In adolescents and adults, the disturbance is manifested by symptoms
such as preoccupation with getting rid of primary and secondary sex
characteristics (e.g., request for hormones, surgery, or other procedures to physically alter sexual characteristics to simulate the other
sex) or belief that he or she was born the wrong sex.

C. The disturbance is not concurrent with a physical intersex condition.

D. The disturbance causes clinically significant distress or impairment in
social, occupational, or other important areas of functioning.[2,A]

The DSM further requires the clinician to include the sexual orientation of the
individual in a diagnosis of GID. In the DSM-III[1] the required specification was
'heterosexual', 'homosexual', 'bisexual', or 'asexual', but eventually the members
of the APA noticed that the terms *homosexual* and *heterosexual* are interpreted
differently if derived from the person's self-identification (from the perspective of
the patient), or from the psychiatrist's external identification. Since the DSM IV-TR
the possible designations have been changed to 'Sexually Attracted to Males',
'Sexually Attracted to Females', 'Sexually Attracted to Both', 'Sexually Attracted
to Neither'[2].

[A] *Legal note: this quote is 351 words in length.*

A.4 The DSM's Transvestic Fetishism, TV

In the DSM IV-TR[2] Transvestic Fetishism [TV] is listed as Condition 302.3. According to the DSM transvestic fetishism can only occur in individuals designated male by medical professionals, who also self-identify as heterosexual.

The DSM IV-TR diagnostic criteria of Transvestic Fetishism are as follows:

A. Over a period of at least 6 months, in a heterosexual male, recurrent, intense sexually arousing fantasies, sexual urges, or behaviors involving cross-dressing.

B. The fantasies, sexual urges, or behaviors cause clinically significant distress or impairment in social, occupational, or other important areas of functioning.[2,A]

The DSM further requires the clinician to specify if Gender Dysphoria has also been diagnosed.

A Legal note: this quote is 46 words in length.

A.5 Glossary

A.5.1 Acronyms

APA

The American Psychiatric Association. The APA consists of approximately 33,000 psychiatric physicians[3]. The APA defines and publishes the DSM.

DSM

The **Diagnostic and Statistical Manual of Mental Disorders**, published by the American Psychiatric Association about every 10 years. The current edition is referred to as DSM-IV-TR.

The DSM provides standard criteria for the classification of what the APA calls "mental disorders". The first edition (in 1952) also officially served to provide billing-codes for psychiatric services to insurance companies, a purpose that is still maintained today. While the DSM contains no statistics, it does contain ample and often detailed descriptions of how to catalogue "mental disorders" according to observed symptoms.

The DSM is not based on science, but on political and professional consensus usually made-up in subcommittees working on various passages of the DSM. consequently, some behaviours are defined as "disorders" in some editions, while the same behaviour is completely missing in another; homosexuality being a prime example.

FtM

An abbreviation for a **Female to Male** trans person. Also FTM or F/M.

GID

GID is an acronym for **Gender Identity Disorder**, a DSM diagnosis. For details, please see A.3, *The DSM's Gender Identity Disorder, GID*.

HRT

Hormone Replacement Therapy, or often Hormone Therapy, is used to approximate female, or male levels of sex hormones (also called sex steroids) in MtF or FtM transsexuals respectively.

For MtF transsexuals HRT usually consists of female hormone supplements (such as estrogens and progestins) and testosterone blockers.

For FtM transsexuals HRT usually consists of testosterone supplements only, no estrogen blockers are necessary.

After removal of the primary reproductive organs (testicles in MtF's and ovaries in FtM's), the drug-intake for HRT can usually be reduced significantly.

MtF

An abbreviation for a **Male to Female** trans person. Also MTF or M/F.

SOC

This abbreviation is often used as a designation for the **Standards Of Care** published by WPATH (see below). The original title of version 6, published in 2000, is [SOC] *The Harry Benjamin International Gender Dysphoria Association's Standards Of Care For Gender Identity Disorders, Sixth Version,* the original title of version 7, published in 2012, is *WPATH Standards of care for the health of transsexual, transgender, and gender nonconforming people.*

SRS

Refers to Sex Reassignment Surgery. This includes genital surgery in either the Male to Female or Female to Male case. Usually the term refers to either a vaginoplasty or a phalloplasty, but can also be used for partial surgeries such as an orchiectomy, a labiaplasty and so on. Any related genital surgery for trans people are restricted by the SOC.

Other suggested designations for SRS include *gender reassignment surgery (GRS)* and *gender alignment surgery*, which are technically wrong as not the gender, but the anatomical sex of an individual is corrected.

Other authors use the term to include any surgical procedure that aligns a person's appearance more to the preferred gender, this can include anything from facial surgery to liposuction to facelifts, hair transplants, or genital surgery. I find this use confusing as the range of surgeries is no longer clearly defined, we find many surgeries people may use for other purposes in this range (e.g. anti-aging procedures). Using the term(s) in such a way also deprives trans communities of a specific umbrella term to designate *genital surgeries,* a need that is often deemed to be unique to trans people.

TV

TV is an acronym for **transvestite**. The term 'transvestite' is usually considered to be a derogatory description for an individual who dresses in the clothes of the 'opposite' gender or sex, although some members of trans communities have reclaimed the former mental-health designation. The original mental health designation was only applied to biological male individuals. Most people who dress in clothes of the 'opposite' gender or sex prefer the term crossdresser, the activity is referred to as crossdressing, drag or drab.

WPATH

Is an acronym for The World Professional Association for Transgender Health.. Their website can be found at http://www.wpath.org/, where various documents, such as the SOC, can be downloaded for free.

WPATH is incorporated in the US, but membership is open for practitioners worldwide. However, most members are based in the US. While WPATH is officially a "not for profit" organization, it is of course heavily involved in the promotion of the (for profit) services of many of its members.

The fact that a 'not for profit' organization can *mandate* the *pay-for* services of its members and still maintain a legal status of *not for profit* is an oxymoron. In fact, this strategy appears to be more of a use of a tax evasion loophole than it is a provision of a public service - which originally was the idea why not for profit organizations were granted special legal privileges.

A.5.2 Terms

Asexual
A person who has no sexual attractions to others.

Bisexual
A person who may feel romantic or sexual attractions to people of both genders or sexs as defined by the gender binary. (in contrast with pansexual).

Cis/Cisgender/Cissexual
For individuals who define 'transgender'/'transsexual' as a self-identification, 'cisgender'/'cissexual' means 'not transgender'/'not transsexual' (formed after heterosexual for 'not homosexual').

The term 'cis' is seen as more inclusive, just as 'trans' is deemed to be more inclusive tan 'transgender' or 'transsexual'.

For individuals who define in particular 'transsexual' as a condition, the term 'cisgender' can be oppressive and exclusionary in that it implies that individuals can never transition to become cis-people, that there is an invisible, but absolute line between a 'trans woman/men' and a 'true women/men' (e.g. cis women/men). This can be seen in the survey when participants describe themselves as "post-transsexual woman" (see 3.3.8, *Gender Self-Identification*), or as "no longer trans" or "never having been transsexual" (see 5.3, *Self-Awareness*)

Crossdresser
Someone who dresses in the clothing of the "opposite" gender or sex, the activity is referred to as crossdressing, drag or drab.

Discrimination
Unfair or prejudicial treatment of individuals or groups. Discrimination prevents equal access. Discrimination may be evident at a systemic level or an individual level.

Gay
A person who feels romantic or sexual attraction to people of the same gender or sex. (See also homosexual).

Gender Binary
The classification of sex and gender into exactly two distinct and disconnected states: male and female. This concept establishes a social boundary and discourages people from crossing or mixing physical or social aspects of the two states.

Gender Expression
The social expression of gender, often shown through clothing, behaviours, interests or names within or beyond the gender binary.

Gender Self-Identification
Our self-identification as female, male, fluid, bi-gender, neither or other.

Gender Identity
Clinical use: a 'diagnosis' if a person 'is' or 'should be' male or female. In the clinical use 'gender identity' is NOT self-identified, but assigned by a professional. Community use: the term gender identity is often used as a synonym for gender self-identification.
Community use: a synonym for gender self-identification

Gender Identity Disorder [GID]
Gender Identity Disorder [GID] is a DSM diagnosis. For details, please see A.3, *The DSM's Gender Identity Disorder, GID.*

Gender Role
The oppressive culturally-specific expectations and restrictions that are placed on a person based on whether they are deemed male or female.

Genderqueer
An umbrella term used proudly by some people to defy gender restrictions and/or to deconstruct gender norms. The term is not reclaimed by everyone and may be hurtful for some. The term is not a synonym for 'transsexual' or 'transgender'.

Heterosexual
A person who is romantically or sexually attracted to people of the other gender or sex. Please note that, historically, a transwomen who was attracted to a female was described as *heterosexual* in the clinical literature.

Homosexual
A person who feels romantic or sexual attraction to people of the same gender or sex. (See also *gay* and *lesbian*.) Please note that, historically, a transwomen who was attracted to a male was described as *homosexual* in the clinical literature.

Internalized Oppression
When members of a marginalized group learn, accept and believe in their inferiority to a dominant group.

Ideology
An ideology is a vision, a set of ideas that describes one's goals, defines one's expectations and actions.

Intersex
An umbrella term defined by clinicians to describe individuals whose biological sex characteristics don't fit their textbook expectations. The clinical definition does not include self-identification or neurological differences as valid descriptors to designate a person as 'intersex'.

-ism
A harmful belief that a group of people are superior to another group of people. Examples include: ageism, anti-Semitism, audism, cis-sexism, classism, ethnocentrism, heterosexism, monosexism, racism, sexism, shadism, sizism... Some -isms have alternative names, for example misogyny/misandry.

Lesbian
A female identified person who feels romantic or sexual attraction to people of the same gender or sex.

Marginalization
Excluding whole groups of people from meaningful participation in social activities.

Misogyny
The hatred of women and 'feminine' characteristics.

Normative
Adheres to implicit or explicit norms or expectations pressured from the outside and controlled from within a social group.

Oppression
The obvious and subtle ways dominant groups unjustly maintain status, privilege and power over others.

Ostracism
Ostracism is an unofficial exclusion of individuals or groups from society through social rejection or deliberate ignorance.

Out
When a person lives openly as gay, lesbian, bisexual or trans.

Pansexual
A person who may feel romantic or sexual attractions to people of any gender or sex.

Paraphilia
A Paraphilia is an intense sexual arousal to atypical objects or situations. Examples of paraphilias include pedophilia, sexual sadism and exhibitionism.

Passing
This is the privilege given to a person who is believed to be a member of a dominant group (i.e., non-trans, cis, white, non-disabled,...). Passing as trans (i.e., believed to be a cis woman) often allows individuals to access services either at all, or with less prejudice.

-Phobia
A learned dislike, fear and/or hatred of a particular group of people. It is expressed through beliefs that devalue, demean and terrorize people. Examples include: biphobia, homophobia, Islamophobia, transphobia, xenophobia...

Physical Transition
The changes trans people use to align their bodies to their self-identification. This can range from hair-removal to hormonal treatment to a variety of surgeries; individual needs vary greatly.

Post-trans
The term 'post-trans' is usually used in conjunction with individuals, i.e. *a post-trans woman* or *a post-trans man.* Individuals who use this terminology generally identify as female or male and have transitioned to a degree that they no longer deem the term 'trans' appropriate. The term can individually be interpreted as 'healed from being trans' (e.g. through transition and medical intervention), or as 'having put trans behind'. Post-trans individuals generally do not, or no longer identify as trans people, however they may continue to use the term 'trans' in certain circumstances to describe their lives, experiences, or social position.

Prejudice
A negative opinion formed about a person or a group of people based on non-factual, preconceived beliefs.

Queer
An umbrella term used proudly by some people to defy gender or sexual restrictions. This is also one way some people identify themselves as members of the lesbian, gay, bi, and/or trans communities or cultures (see 'genderqueer'). The term is defined differently in relation to culture, individual experiences and expressions, is not reclaimed by everyone and may be hurtful for some.

Questioning
A person who is trying to find out how to identify, usually either in relation to sexual orientation or gender self-identification.

Sex

A label given by a government approved 'experts' to describe the physical body as male or female. If given at birth, external genitals are usually taken as reference, later in life genetics, hormonal levels, internal reproductive organs or physical development may be used by other 'experts'. The opinions of these various 'experts' need not be identical.

Sexual Orientation

The emotional, romantic and sexual attraction to another person(s). Sexual orientation can change over time. Sexual orientation can be different from actual sexual behaviour. Sexual orientations can be complex.

Social Transition

The visible part of socially changing gender roles. This usually includes dress, behaviour, language and can include physical markers, such as hair length.

Stealth

When a trans person is not 'out' as trans in some or all of their social circles (friends, employers, colleagues).

Trans

An umbrella term for a person whose gender self-identification does not match society's expectations. (See also *post-trans.*)

Transvestite

The term 'transvestite' is usually considered to be a derogatory description for an individual who dresses in the clothes of the 'opposite' gender or sex, although some members of trans communities have reclaimed the former mental-health designation. The original mental health designation was only applied to biological male individuals. Most people who dress in clothes of the 'opposite' gender or sex prefer the term crossdresser, the activity is referred to as crossdressing, drag or drab.

Transvestitism

Transvestitism is a short form of the DSM's diagnosis Transvestic Fetishism (for details, see A.4, *The DSM's Transvestic Fetishism, TV*).

Trans Man (FTM)

A female-to-male trans person.

Trans Woman (MTF)

A male-to-female trans person.

Transition

The process trans people go through to overcome physical, legal and social barriers so they can express their self-identified gender.

Two-spirit

A term based on interpretation of words used in different Aboriginal cultures to refer to a person having both a male and female spirit. It can include Anglo/North American ideas of both sexual orientation and gender identity (i.e., both a gay cis man and a trans-man could claim the identity of two-spirit man). It also includes significant spiritual and cultural layers.

A.6 References

[1] APA. (1980). *Diagnostic and statistical manual of mental disorders, third edition, DSM-III.* The American Psychiatric Association.

[2] APA. (2000). *Diagnostic and statistical manual of mental disorders, fourth edition, text revision, DSM-IV-TR.* The American Psychiatric Association.

[3] APA. The American Psychiatric Association website, About the APA. http://www.psychiatry.org/about-apa--psychiatry.

[4] Benjamin, H. (1966). *The Transsexual Phenomenon; a Scientific Report on Transsexualism and Sex Conversion in the Human Male and Female.* ASIN B001T8IAGI.

[5] Bering, J. (2010). The Third Gender. *Scientific American Mind, 2010*(5).

[6] Blanchard, R. (1989). The concept of autogynephilia and the typology of male gender dysphoria. *Journal of Nervous & Mental Disease 177*(10).

[7] Blanton, D. A. & Cook, L. M. (2002). *They Fought Like Demons: Women Soldiers in the American Civil War.* Louisiana State University Press. ISBN 978-08071-2806-0.

[8] Bornstein, K. (1995). *Gender Outlaw: On Men, Women, and the Rest of Us.* New York. Vintage. ISBN 978-0679-75701-6.

[9] Butler, J. (1989). *Gender trouble: Feminism and the Subversion of Identity.* Routledge. ISBN 978-0415-90043-0.

[10] Butler, J. (2004). *Undoing Gender.* Routledge. ISBN 978-0415-96923-9.

[11] California. (2012). *California Senate Bill No. 1172.* An act to add Article 15 to Chapter 1 of Division 2 of the Business and Professions Code, relating to healing arts: Sexual orientation change efforts. http://leginfo.legislature.ca.gov/faces/billAnalysisClient.xhtml.

[12] Canada. (1867). *The Canadian Constitution.* The Constitution Act, 1867. http://laws-lois.justice.gc.ca/eng/Const/page-1.html.

[13] Canada. (1982). *Canadian Charter of Rights and Freedoms. The Constitution Act, 1982.* http://laws-lois.justice.gc.ca/eng/Const/PRINT_E.pdf.

[14] Cole, M. L. & Rounsley, A. (1996). *True Selves: Understanding Transsexualism.* ISBN: 978-0787-96702-4.

[15] Courvant, D. (1999). Coming Out Disabled: A Transsexual Woman Considers Queer Contributions to Living with Disability. *International Journal of Sexuality and Gender Studies 4*(1).

[16] Diamond, L. M., Pardo, S. T., Butterworth, M. R. (2011). Transgender Experience and Identity. In *Handbook of Identity Theory and Research.* Schwartz, S. J. et al. Eds. DOI 10.1007/978-1-4419-7988-9_26

[17] Dispenza, F., Watson, L. B., Chung, Y. B., Brack, G. (2012). Experience of career-related discrimination for female-to-male transgender persons: a qualitative study. *The Career Development Quarterly 60*(1).

[18] Dreger, A., Feder E. K., Tamar-Mattis, A. (2012). Prenatal dexamethasone for congenital adrenal hyperplasia: an ethics canary in the modern medical mine. *Journal of Bioethical Inquiry 9*(3). DOI 10.1007/s11673-012-9384-9.

[19] Ehrensaft, D. (2008). Raising girlyboys: A parent's perspective. *Studies in Gender & Sexuality 8*(3).

[20] Ekins, R. (2005). Science, Politics and Clinical Intervention: Harry Benjamin, Transsexualism and the Problem of Heteronormativity. *Sexualities, 8*(3).

21 Elliot, P. (2009). Engaging Trans Debates on Gender Variance: A Feminist Analysis. *Sexualities, 12*(1).

22 Elliot, P. (2010). *Debates in Transgender, Queer and Feminist Theory.* Ashgate Publishing. ISBN 978-1409-40394-4.

23 Escoffier, J. (2011). Imagining the she/male: pornography and the transsexualization of the heterosexual male. *Studies in Gender and Sexuality, 12*(4).

24 Feinberg, L. (1996). *Transgender warriors: Making history from Joan of Arc to Dennis Rodman. Boston.* Beacon Press. ISBN 978-0807-07941-6.

25 Feinberg, L. (1998). *Trans Liberation: Beyond Pink or Blue.* Beacon Press. ISBN 978-0807-07951-5.

26 Finkel, A. (2006). *Social Policy and Practice in Canada, a History.* Wilfrid Laurier University Press. ISBN: 978-0-88920-475-1.

27 Foucault, M. (1988). *The History of Sexuality, Vol. 3: The Care of the Self.* ISBN: 978-0394-74155-0.

28 Freund, K., Steiner, B. W., Chan, S. (1982). Two types of cross-gender identity. *Archives of Sexual Behavior 11*(1).

29 Gansler, L. L. (2005). *The Mysterious Private Thompson: The Double Life of Sarah Emma Edmonds, Civil War Soldier.* Free Press. ISBN 978-07432-4280-6.

30 Greatheart, M. S. (2010). *The Fred Study: stories of life satisfaction and wellness from post-transition transgender men.* Unpublished Masters Thesis. Faculty of Graduate Studies, University of British Columbia (Vancouver, BC).

31 Halberstam, J. (1998). *Female Masculinity.* Duke University Press. ISBN: 978-0822-32243-6.

32 Hausman, B. L. (1995). *Changing Sex: Transsexualism, Technology, and the Idea of Gender.* Duke University Press. ISBN 978-0822-31680-0.

33 Hausman, B. L. (2001). Recent Transgender Theory. *Feminist Studies 27*(2).

34 Hertzer, K. (1999). *Mann oder Frau - Wenn die Grenzen fliessend werden.* ISBN: 978-3720-52063-8.

35 Hirschfeld, M. (1904). *Berlins Drittes Geschlecht.* ISBN: 3-921-49559-8.

36 Hirschfeld, M. (1905). Geschlechtsübergänge. *Monatsschrift für Harnkrankheiten und Sexuelle Hygiene.*

37 Hirschfeld, M. (1930). *Geschlechtskunde. Auf Grund dreissigjähriger Forschung und Erfahrung bearbeitet.* 5 Bände. Berlin & Stuttgart, Püttmann 1926 - 1930.

38 Jeffrey, D. (2002). *A Terrain of Struggle: Reading Race in Social Work Education.* ISBN 978-0612-69243-5. University of Toronto Press.

39 Johnson, K. (2007). Changing sex, changing self. *Men and Masculinities 10*(1).

40 Keller, S. E. (1999). Operations of legal rhetoric: examining transsexual and judicial identity. *Harvard Civil Rights-Civil Liberties Law Review, 34*(2).

41 Kerrigan, M. F. (2011). Transgender discrimination in the military: the new don't ask, don't tell. *Psychology, Public Policy, and Law 18*(3). Advance online publication. DOI: 10.1037/a0025771.

42 KJV. (1611). *The King James Bible.*

43 Lawrence, A. (2007). Becoming what we love: Autogynephilic transsexualism conceptualized as an expression of romantic love. *Perspectives in Biology and Medicine 50*(4). PMID 17951885.

44 Lloyd, A. W. (2005). Defining the human: Are transgender people strangers to the law? *Berkeley Journal of Gender, Law & Justice, 20.*

[45] Lok, V. & Chapman, S. (2009). *The Mental Health Workforce in California*. UCSF Center for the Health Professions. http://www.futurehealth.ucsf.edu/Content/29/2009-03_The_Mental_Health_Workforce_in_California_Trends_in_Employment_Education_and_Diversity.pdf.

[46] Lombardi, E. (2009). Varieties of transgender/transsexual lives and their relationship with transphobia. *Journal of Homosexuality 56*(8). DOI 10.1080/00918360903275393.

[47] Lurkhur, K. A. (2010). Medieval Silence and Modern Transsexuality. *Studies in Gender and Sexuality 11*(4).

[48] Mandlis, L. R. (2011). Whose crazy investment in sex? *Journal of Homosexuality, 58*(2). DOI 10.1080/00918369.2011.540177.

[49] Martin, K. A. (2007). Transsexualism: Clinical guide to gender identity disorder. *Journal of Family Practice 6*(2).

[50] Mayeda, J. (2005). Re-imagining feminist theory: transgender identity, feminism, and the law. *Canadian Journal of Women and the Law, 17*(2).

[51] Moffat, K. (2001). *A Poetics of Social Work: Personal Agency and Social Transformation in Canada, 1920-1939*. ISBN 978-0802-04860-8. University of Toronto Press.

[52] Money, J. (1974). *Man and Woman, Boy and Girl: Differentiation and Dimorphism of Gender Identity From Conception to Maturity*. ISBN 978-0801-81406-8. John Hopkins University Press.

[53] Money, J. (1986). *Lovemaps: Clinical Concepts of Sexual/Erotic Health and Pathology, Paraphilia, and Gender Transposition in Childhood, Adolescence, and Maturity*. ISBN: 0-8264-0852-4.

[54] Money, J. (1994). *Sex Errors of the Body and Related Syndromes: A Guide to Counseling Children, Adolescents, and Their Families*. ISBN: 978-155-766150-0.

[55] Money, J. & Ehrhardt, A. (1996). *Man & Woman, Boy & Girl: Gender Identity from Conception to Maturity*. ISBN: 978-1568-21812-0.

[56] Moser, E. C. (2007). *A Matter of Life - When Gender Doesn't Work*. Lulu Press. ISBN 978-0557-01391-3.

[57] Moser, E. C. (2010). *Manufacturing Insanity: Vol. 1 - Creating Truth / When Darkness Falls*. Lulu Press. ISBN 978-0-557-68916-3.

[58] Moser, E. C. (2010). *Manufacturing Insanity: Vol. 2 - Dangerous Knowledge / The Next Religious War*. Lulu Press. ISBN 978-0-557-68917-0.

[59] Moser, E. C. (2013). Practice Research Paper: Defining Ourselves: *Transsexual and Transgender Individuals Describe Their Experience Of Being Trans*. York University, Department of Graduate Studies, School of Social Work.

[60] Moser, E. C. (2014). Why We Don't Exist: Colonized Bodies, Colonized Minds, Erased Lives - Challenging the Imperialistic Dogma Of 'The Common Transsexual'. ISBN 978-1-304-46904-5. In Print.

[61] Namaste, V. (2000). *Invisible Lives: The Erasure of Transsexual and Transgender People*. Chicago University Press. ISBN 978-0226-56810-2.

[62] Namaste, V. (2005). *Sex Change, Social Change: Reflections on Identity, Institutions, and Imperialism*. Women's Press. ISBN 978-0889-61483-3.

[63] NTCE & NGLTF. (2009). National Transgender Discrimination Survey. *The National Center for Transgender Equality and The National Gay and Lesbian Task Force*. http://www.thetaskforce.org/downloads/reports/fact_sheets/transsurvey_prelim_findings.pdf.

[64] NTCE & NGLTF. (2010). National Transgender Discrimination Survey: Report on Healthcare. *The National Center for Transgender Equality and The National Gay and Lesbian Task Force*. http://transequality.org/PDFs/NTDSReportonHealth_final.pdf.

[65] Orwell, G. (1945). Animal Farm. ISBN 0-452-28424-4.

[66] Prosser, J. (1998). *Second Skins: The Body Narratives of Transsexuality.* New York: Columbia University Press. ISBN 978-0231-10935-2.

[67] Raymond, J. G. (1979). *The Transsexual Empire: The Making of the She-Male.* Teachers College. ISBN 978-0807-76272-1.

[68] Rossiter, A. (2011). Unsettled social work: the challenge of Levinas's ethics. *British Journal of Social Work 41*(5). Doi:10.1093/bjsw/bcr004.

[69] RSV. (2006). *The Holy Bible, Revised Standard Edition.* Second Catholic Edition 2006.

[70] Sakomoto, I. (2003). Changing images and similar dynamics: historical patterning of foreignness in the social work profession. In *The Concept of the Foreign: An Interdisciplinary Dialogue.* Saunders, R., Eds. ISBN 978-0739-10408-8. Lexington Books.

[71] Serano, J. (2007). *Whipping Girl: A Transsexual Woman on Sexism and the Scapegoating of Femininity.* Seal Press. ISBN: 978-1580-05154-5.

[72] Singh, A. A., Hays, D. G., Watson, L. S. (2011). Strength in the face of adversity: resilience strategies of transgender individuals. *Journal of Counseling & Development 89*(1).

[73] Stone, S. (1996). *The Empire Strikes Back: A Posttranssexual Manifesto.* In Body Guards: Cultural Politics of Gender Ambiguity. Routledge. ISBN 978-0415-90388-2.

[74] Stryker, S. (1994). My words to Victor Frankenstein above the village of Chamounix: Performing transgender rage. *GLQ: Journal of Lesbian & Gay Studies, 1*(3)

[75] Taylor, J. (2011). The Intimate Insider: negotiating the ethics of friendship when doing insider research. *Qualitative Research 11*(1).

[76] TransPulse. (2009). *The TransPulse Survey.* http://transpulseproject.ca/. Various reports are available at http://transpulseproject.ca/research-type/e-bulletin/.

[77] Urban, M. (2009). Transsexualism or delusions of sex change? Avoiding misdiagnosis. *Psychiatria Polska 43*(6). PMID: 20209883.

[78] Wong, Y-L. R, Cheng, S., Choi, S-Y. (2003). Deconstructing culture in cultural competence: aissenting voices from Asian-Canadian practitioners. *Canadian Social Work Review 20*(2).

[79] WPATH. (2001). The Harry Benjamin international gender dysphoria association's standards of care for gender identity disorders, sixth version. *The World Professional Association for Transgender Health.* http://www.wpath.org/publications_standards.cfm.

[80] WPATH. (2012). Standards of care for the health of transsexual, transgender, and gender nonconforming people. *The World Professional Association for Transgender Health.* http://www.wpath.org/publications_standards.cfm.

[81] Yee, J. Y. & Dumbrill, G. C. (2003) *Whiteout: looking for race in Canadian social work practice. Multicultural Social Work in Canada: Working with Diverse Ethno-racial Communities.* Al-Krewnawi, A. & Graham, J. R. (eds). Oxford University Press. Toronto, Canada.

[82] Zucker, K. J. (2005). Gender Identity Disorder in Children and Adolescents. *Annual Review of Clinical Psychology 1*.

[83] Zucker, K. J. (2008). Children with gender identity disorder: Is there a best practice?. *Neuropsychiatrie De l'Enfance Et De l'Adolescence, 56*(6).

[84] Zucker, K. J., & Lawrence, A. A. (2009). Epidemiology of gender identity disorder: recommendations for the standards of care of The World Professional Association for Transgender Health. International Journal of Transgenderism, 11(1). Doi:10.1080/15532730902799946.

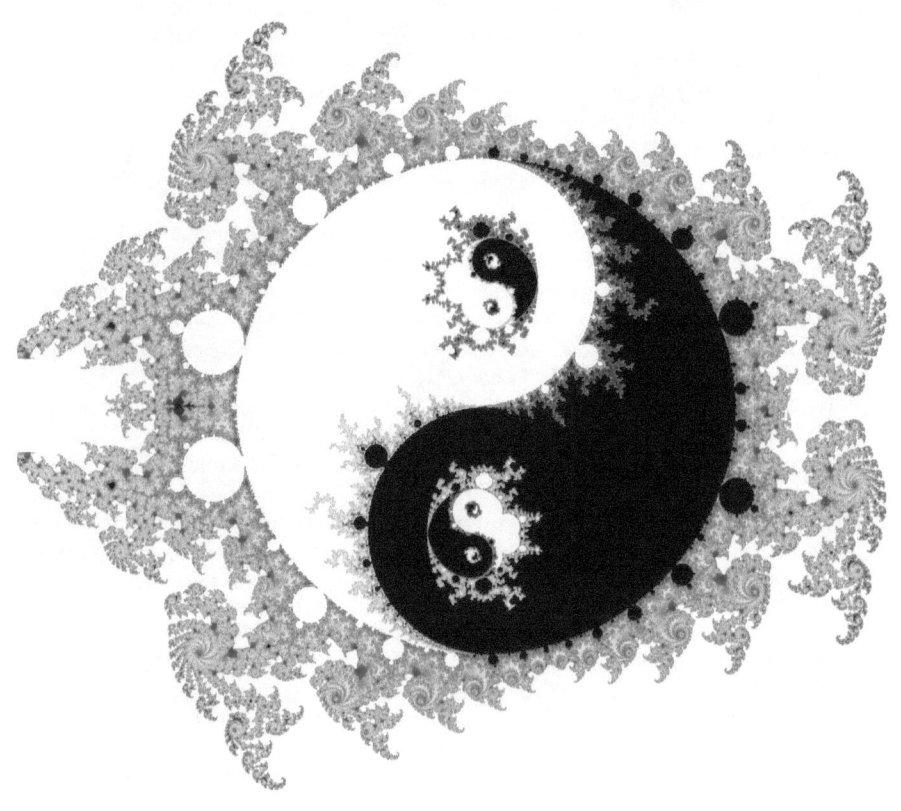

Diversity makes our world beautiful.

Our world exists because of it, through it, and for it.

We all are this diversity.